A Chosen LIFE Study

Ephesians 1:3-8

Praise be to the God And Father of our Lord Jesus Christ, who has blessed us in the heavenly realms with every spiritual blessing in Christ. **For He chose us in Him** before the creation of the world to be holy and blameless in His sight. In love He predestined us to be adopted as His sons through Jesus Christ, in accordance with His pleasure and will...**To be the praise of His glorious grace, which He has freely given us in the one He loves.** In Him we have redemption through His blood, the forgiveness of sins, in accordance with the riches of God's grace that He lavished on us with all wisdom and understanding.

AUTHOR BOB BOWMAN

'for I will fight those who fight you, and I will save your children' Isaiah 49:25

authorHOUSE®

AuthorHouse™
1663 Liberty Drive
Bloomington, IN 47403
www.authorhouse.com
Phone: 1-800-839-8640

First published by AuthorHouse   3/18/2010

ISBN: 978-1-4490-0122-3 (e)
ISBN: 978-1-4490-0123-0 (sc)

Printed in the United States of America
Bloomington, Indiana

This book is printed on acid-free paper.

INTRODUCTION TO A CHOSEN LIFE STUDY

During this volatile time in world history, do you long for genuine peace and joy in your life?

Does your heart cry out to know

- *that God is real?*

- *that Jesus Christ can change your life?*

- *that the Holy Spirit is active and moving in lives today?*

- *that God really does care and have a plan for your life?*

In this book, A Chosen Life Study, author Bob Bowman, compassionately imparts the life journey Jesus has chosen for him. As his body lay alone and covered in cow manure, Bob cried out to God. Later that night, lying in a hospital bed, Bob surrendered his life to Jesus Christ and declared, "God, today I died, My life is over. I ask you to say goodbye to my pregnant wife, and you gave me life instead. So, (now) today it belongs to you." His words rose as a sweet aroma to God, and Bob was moved to tell the world of God's saving love.

Bob uses prose, poetry, inspired hymns, and words of scripture to reveal that God has indeed chosen each one of us who will believe on His Son and gives practical direction on how to travel the God-directed paths for our own lives. His message is simple, but it demonstrates that before time God purposed your life to be unique and that you are of infinite worth to Him.

According to John the Beloved, "the whole world would not have room for the books that would be written" about the things that Jesus did. A Chosen Life Study contains one such story of what He is doing to change lives today.

We must have constant regard to the word of God, as the rule of our actions, and the spring of our comforts; and have it in our thoughts night and day. For this purpose no time is amiss. (Ps 1:4-6)

BOB BOWMAN, a retired restaurateur and farmer, semi driver for short distances, and his wife, Sylvia, live in central Iowa where they enjoy visits with their seven children and their families.

Author's suggestion. I recommend that each reader have note pad, pencil and bible near them to jot down verses as well as thoughts, as you dig deep into God's word to you.

A CHOSEN LIFE STUDY

1. *Do your best to present yourself to God as one approved, a worker who does not need to be ashamed and who correctly handles the word of truth. (*<u>2 Timothy 2:15</u> *)*

2. *2.We must have constant regard to the word of God, as the rule of our actions, and the spring of our comforts; and have it in our thoughts night and day. For this purpose no time is amiss. (*<u>Ps 1:4-6</u>*)*

3. *3.The name of the LORD is a fortified tower;*
    the righteous run to Him and are safe. (<u>Proverbs 18:10</u>*)*

4. *4. Study verses:* <u>Eccl.12:12</u>

5. *Now all has been heard; here is the conclusion of the matter: Fear God and keep his commandments, for this is the [duty] of every human being.*

Morning Devotion

Ephesians 2:6-10 (New International Version - UK)

And God raised *us* up with Christ and seated us with him in the heavenly realms in Christ Jesus, in order that in the coming ages he might show the incomparable riches of his grace, expressed in his kindness to *us* in Christ Jesus. For it is by grace *you* have been saved, through faith— and this *not from yourselves*, it isthe gift of God—not by works, so that *no-one can boast*. *For we are God's workmanship, created in Christ Jesus to do good works, which God prepared in advance for us to do.*

1 Thessalonians 2:8 *8 We loved you so much that we were delighted to share with you not only the gospel of God but our lives as well, because you had become so dear to us.*

I Come to you in His Glory, relative to His Words:

That all men may be blessed.....

In the name of the Father, the Son, and the Holy Spirit.

Isaiah Chapter nine Verses one through Seven

For God's Eternal Glory

1. Nevertheless, there will be no more gloom for those who were in darkness. In the past He humbled the land of Zebulun and the land of Naphatali, but in the future He will honor Galilee, by the way of the sea, along the Jordon---

2. The people walking in darkness have seen a great light; on those living in the land of deep darkness a light has dawned.

3. You have enlarged the nation and increased their joy; they rejoice before you as people rejoice at the harvest, as soldiers rejoice when dividing the plunder.

4. For as in the day of Midian's defeat, you have shattered the yoke that burdens them, the bar across their shoulders, the rod of their oppressor.

5. Every warrior's boot used in battle and every garment rolled in blood will be destined for burning, will be fuel for the fire.

6. **For to us a child is born, to us a son is given, and the government will be on his shoulders. And he will be called Wonderful Counselor, Mighty God, Everlasting Father, Prince of Peace.**

7. Of the increase of his government and peace there will be no end. He will reign on David's throne and over his kingdom, establishing and upholding it with justice and righteousness from that time on and forever. The zeal of the LORD Almighty will accomplish this.

Table of Contents

"How it all started for me!"

Although I am a gentile, I came into the Kingdom of God when Jesus told me: You must be born again, then I heard Him say, I tell you the truth, Bob, unless, you are born again, you cannot see the Kingdom Of God. That day when He spoke those words to me I was so excited as I listened. Then Jesus replied, "I assure you, Bob, no one can enter the Kingdom Of God without being born of water and the Spirit. Humans can reproduce only human life, but the Holy Spirit gives birth to spiritual life. (Not beyond anyone's understanding, Bob) So don't be surprised when I say, You must be born again. The wind blows wherever it wants. Just as you can hear the wind but can't tell where it comes from or where it is going, so you can't explain how people are born of the Spirit." (What can I do, Lord Jesus,) Check Out… **Revelation 3:19-20, and certainly John 3:3-8** These instructions were not given immediate attention, but they enlarged my spirit of understanding, and bless the Lord He never released me till the narrow road became clear.

(My life and my life's story is like the one as recorded here in the book of Amos…Chapter 7:14-16

Amos answered Amaziah, "I was neither a prophet or a prophet's son, but I was a shepherd, and I also took care of sycamore-fig trees. (Farming for me) But the Lord took me from tending the flock and said to me, Go, prophecy to my people Israel, now then, hear the word of the Lord, You say, Do not prophesy against Israel, And stop preaching against the house of Isaac."

The layout of this book has obviously passed through my mind and heart. I use many scriptures because the Holy Spirit has called them to my attention. The scriptures are numerous because whatever is said, is said best by our Father in heaven. My voice is naturally smaller, and lacks His magnetism. (His power to call) However, if you hear His voice (word), no matter who speaks it, you are accountable to it, because in His wisdom and power He wants you to be His child. (Born again)

I grew up in a family, the fourth of eight children. We were an average Midwestern American farm family, Most of our lives was spent in and around the farm, or small town environment. Farming, growing corn and livestock were very familiar activities which created much of our family income. Money was always tight – It was a struggle for survival, but it didn't cause a lack for the things we really needed. Somehow, a happy love was always close to our hearts, and we somehow realized that God was responsible for that.

My mother was a great cook, a very good listener with a loving and forgiving heart. My father was also dedicated and loving but was very busy supporting our large family. He loved the livestock business and many times he would be away from home, out in most of the western states, for long periods of time buying cattle that he could resell close to home.

As I have already made known to you, we were a family born into the country life style, and educated in small time American schools, However, most of the children received our high school education in one of the largest schools in the state of Iowa at Davenport High School. While I'm on the subject, I married a small town country girl, and we have had the Lord's blessing with seven children born into the country style of living that we all enjoyed.

It is easy for me to share those precious times, but more than that, I would like to share with you a more lasting and wonderful experience that I have been blessed with. A much larger Family Of God. The one that Christ established at the Cross of Calvary. He poured out His precious blood for eternal rewards, for all believers.

Since the time of my first conscious awareness of God, I can testify that I have always believed and loved the Lord Jesus. But I can tell the world that for the first forty-one years of my life I was lost and headed straight for hell, while believing with all my heart that I was going to heaven. Inwardly, I thought I was a good person; I was baptized and went through confirmation. I attended church and was a church member. My trust was centered on my own life, and not His. After committing my life to Jesus I understood his words in Proverbs 14:12 which reads: "There is a way that seems right to a man, but the end thereof is the ways of death."

I, like my father, became involved as a livestock dealer, owning and operating a business of my own. Cleaning stockyard pens was a must operation, and I operated a small skid-loader to accomplish this job.

One day, as I was operating my small skid-loader tractor, I committed a careless mistake, one that trapped me between life and death. The arm of the loader pinned me against the frame of the tractor shutting off my supply of oxygen. I realized then, more than ever before, our need for God's special gift of fresh air, and how he sustains us each day, without our even giving Him Thanks for this life sustaining gift. As I lay there dying, I didn't even give Him thanks for the life he had sustained for forty one years, along with all the other special blessings I had received from his bountiful and abundant hand of mercy, His love, and His sacrifice.

I remember just a few of the thoughts that invaded my mind, leaving me without peace. Thoughts like this one: So this is where I die? *Of all the deaths that I had ever imagined, I never thought of it being in pen four, or even the stockyards, where I spent most of my days and some of my nights, buying livestock, and then chasing the livestock onto trucks for shipment to various places in Iowa and distant states. The stockyards where I employed myself didn't smell anymore…It was death that I was now smelling.* While it seemed to move closer, I am persuaded that God Almighty alone gave me this thought: How can your wife, Sylvia, raise the five boys by herself; with our first girl due to be born in just two short months. Among my frenzied thoughts came this thought, along with his power to fulfill it: "Let me say goodbye", spoken with this paralyzing thought…*If she would just walk down the aisle, which had a much different smell than the aisle we walked down together that February day in 1959, so I could wave to her… maybe even mutter the word's, Sorry!…Take Care! It seemed that wish was all that I had left and would satisfy the pain in my heart for causing the separation of me, from my dear family. You can take it from me; "How lacking we are with our prayers." When His real desire is to give us so much more for our prayer's content.*

The result of that prayer has bestowed on me an additional 38 years of life while living a new life with my wife and family in this world.

While even now anticipating a greater blessing from God. At the young age of 78, *I am now anticipating the joy of living a life, through Jesus Christ our Lord, serving Him in the glory that He so richly deserves, through Jesus Christ His Son, our Lord and Savior. To Him belongs all praise.*

As we keep drawing closer to the Almighty we understand that He has plans of His own that include us, and He uses special messengers to carry them out. Even before the prayers left my mind, He was answering them. Instantly I felt all the hydraulic pressure that was crushing me, release…..freeing my arm. My hand reached for the key to the tractor, which at the slightest turn sent me speeding through a gate to the alley in the stock yards that I had prayed my wife would show herself. Instantly I crashed into a fence, and just as quickly my best friend came upon the scene and being a man of many talents, placed himself in the operator's seat and raised the hydraulic system into a higher place and I began gasping for air. He pulled me out into a liquid pool of manure, then hurried to my office to call an ambulance. Dripping with that smelling fertilizer that only livestock can produce, they hurried me off in an ambulance to the emergency room of the hospital, where hours later I received the first good news that I had heard in what seemed like an eternity. I had received broken ribs that would in God's time be healed……another gift from God. And the gifts kept coming. Later that night with my family surrounding the bed, I heard His small voice for the first time: "You said, let me say goodbye". I answered for the first time. 'But Lord, I'm going to be O. K.' Then after all my family went home, my first true response to God happened with these words that I will always believe he spoke through me….."God, today I died; my life is over…. Little did I realize it was just the beginning of a 'New Life.'

The rest of my life is yours, Jesus." **Amazing words, to say the least;** spoken through the heart of a person who had not yet recognized his sins. Yet, His Spirit hovered over my life, until in His mercy, purpose and timing, He allowed me to flow from this world into His courts of wisdom and understanding with thanksgiving in my heart, where He kept it glowing with His presence, and His promises. *My overview since then has always been that I knew in the abundance of His love, that it was much more than a tractor accident that had taken its place in my heart and life.* I was beginning to understand His words in Psalm 100 where He calls everyone of His own to faith in His name. *"Shout for joy to the Lord, all the earth worship the Lord with gladness"*

Did I deserve to know Him and trust Him for my life and its salvation? Absolutely not! It was strictly His mercy and my need. He knew better than I what my exact needs were, and what it would take to change the direction of my life. Also, where I could find every Word He ever spoke filled with His grace, mercy and peace! He taught these verses as below.

My mystery! Unknown until He opened my eyes and took me with His gentile hand and patiently led me to *Romans 9:16-17 & 22-26 My calling: 'Yet preaching the Good News is not something I can boast about. I am compelled by God to do it. How terrible for me if I didn't preach the Good News!' 1 Corinthians 9:16.....* My calling? And I Praise Him, for everyone He is calling through our family.

I began immediately to seek God's direction and glorious will, and how it related to this life that I had just committed to Him. I listened intently as our pastor proclaimed His message each Sunday morning in church. ***Oh my joy; that I would listen so intently while earnestly seeking some order from the Lord that I could put into proper focus as a command to me from Jesus. 'Marching orders, if you will has always been a link to my growing in Christ. One that sponsors the joy of my life.***

That vein of living alone is something I look back on as the beginning of life with the Holy Spirit. Yet, It seemed like He never spoke to me enough with orders for the direction of my life. My listening ears were groaning for His commands. But, how wonderfully He kept me. I just couldn't possibly stop listening for Him! As I listened I understood things like "Teach a Sunday school class, and I had many classes to choose from, as all five of our boy's attended Sunday school classes. I started with the oldest one assuring myself of sharing God's love with all of them in a church setting. It certainly was one of the gifted joys' of my entire life. A blessing I will never forget, and I hope they won't either.

It was also a stepping stone for memorizing bible verses, as well as learning how to speak to God in prayer. Both of these marvelous gifts consumed me, leading me into a personal relationship with Our Lord. That walk, although supernatural has been the most natural happening in my life. I really couldn't be myself without it, and I shudder as I consider what my life would have been like if my old self would have continued to control me.

Do I have two lives? One physical and one spiritual. Of course, but which one am I feeding the most?

At this time in my spiritual journey I was very thin in my spiritual body.....Very unstable in mind and spirit, and without the understanding of my real purpose in life. Still, without a firm grip in the Lord, I didn't have that one certain reason for praising God, until He filled me fully with His Spirit. *Knowing that my sins were forgiven..... placed as far as the east is from the west, and that God would remember them no more, plus, a salvation that only Jesus can provide seemed to overwhelm me; And all of this through constant searching for His will.*

The wonderful freedom of living with God forever, abiding with His Son, shouting from the core of my being, that God was my savior and hope, through Jesus our crucified Savior, seemed beyond my hope and vision, but something that I was committed to share with the world. His Spirit was victorious as He transformed me into one of His very own; *depending on His every word for life.* Jesus told His disciples, 'I have food you know not of.' And yes, God passed that food on to us in His word.

In **2 Corinthians 5:19-21** He tells us*: **God was in Christ, making peace between the world and Himself. In Christ God did not hold the world guilty of its sins. And He gave us this message of peace. So we have been sent to speak for Christ. It is as if God is calling to you through us. We speak for Christ when we beg you to be at peace with God. Christ had no sin, but God made Him become sin so that in Christ we could become right with God.***

The Dedication of the Temple

When Solomon finished making these prayers and petitions to the Lord, he stood up in front of the altar of the Lord, where he had been kneeling with his hands raised toward heaven. He stood and in a loud voice blessed the entire congregation of Israel:

"Praise the Lord who has given rest to His people Israel, just as He promised. Not one word has failed of all the wonderful promises He gave through His servant Moses. May the Lord our God be with us as He was with our ancestors; may He never leave us or abandon us. May He give us the desire to do his will in everything and to obey all the commands, decrees, and regulations that He gave our ancestors. And may these words that I have prayed in the presence of the Lord stay before Him constantly, day and night, so that the Lord our God may give justice to me and to His people Israel, according to each day's needs. Then people all over the earth will know that the Lord alone is God and there is no other. And may you be completely faithful to the Lord our God. May you always obey His decrees and commands, just as you are doing today."

1 Kings 8:54-61

And when He (Holy Spirit) comes, He will convict the world of its sin, and of God's righteousness, and of the coming judgment. The world's sin is that it refuses to believe in Me. Judgment will come because the ruler of this world (Satan) has already been judged. **John 16:8-11**

I know that when I come to you, I will come in the full measure of the blessing of Christ….. Romans 15:29

No weapon forged against you will prevail, and you will refute every tongue that accuses you. This is the heritage of the servants of the Lord, and this is their vindication from me, declares the Lord. **Isaiah 54:17**

Is not this the kind of fasting I have chosen: to loose the chains of injustice and untie the cords of the yoke, to set the oppressed free and break every yoke.

Isaiah 58:6 No slave has a permanent place in the family, but a son belongs to it for ever. So if the Son sets you free, you will be free indeed. John 8:35-36

Foreword by Pastor Jon

As a Pastor and friend, it is a great privilege to write this forward for Bob Bowman, a dear brother in the Lord. I am reminded of the apostle Paul when he writes, "I thank my God every time I remember you. In all my prayers for all of you, I always pray with joy because of your partnership in the gospel from the first day until now…" (Philippians 1:3-5). Indeed, the love I have for this man is great and the thankfulness that I have toward the Lord for allowing our paths to cross is even greater.

I have known Bob for quite a while, but it was only about a year ago that we began to really grow close and I began to see his heart for Jesus and those He loves. Indeed we have become close friends. However, the story you will find in the pages that follow is ironically not so much a story of Bob Bowman but rather a story of the grace and mercy of our Lord and Savior, Jesus Christ. I pray that as you read this book, you will begin to see portions of your own life…..your needs, your heartaches, your victories, and your destiny. The Apostle Paul goes on in that great letter to the Philippians to say, "Being confident of this, that he who began a good work in you will carry it on to completion until the day of Christ Jesus." (Philippians 1:6)

After reading this book , I pray that you can be confident of where Jesus Christ is leading you.

May God Bless You.

In Christ, Pastor Jon Wiest

jwiest@radiantonline.org

Special page of interest.

As you read "A Chosen Life Study" you will notice it is not only a story, but a study guide for Christians and non-Christians alike. It presents places where the reader can dig into his own thoughts about the subject matter being discussed, as in: 'Reaching for Righteousness… In The Light Of The Son.' Give special praise as you see where the light is coming from. Righteousness is a word that God includes many times in His Word to make known to the readers that the doors of heaven are wide open to all who have become righteous through repentance in the shed-blood of His Son.

For that reason we use many of the biblical truths to lay a format for readers to flow with the Spirit, into their journey with God the Father through our Lord Jesus Christ…..Think "Shed Blood" of Jesus Christ, and if you were the only person living in this world, He would have still come to Calvary to shed His Blood for you, because God had determined in old testament times that the blood of animals would not provide salvation. Now let's look farther into His life saving word in Hebrews. In fact, the law requires that nearly everything be made clean with blood. Without the shedding of blood, no one can be forgiven. Check out John 19:30 when Jesus spoke the words "It Is Finished." No one can understand God's thought's without God's Spirit. And, no one can receive God's Spirit without first receiving Jesus into their heart. Hebrews 9:22

An amazing truth, therefore, is that He knows every step of our journey and is ever present to help us complete our walk with the Holy Spirit. That He would know who we are… righteous or unrighteous as we depart from this life is proof of that. You may want to study this truthful point hard, and deep as you meditate on His word to you in the study of this book. Incorporate your name into the verses as you read them, to see if you are answering, or denying His plea. For example let's use the name Bob, to find how one becomes righteous. (It would be helpful to go back to page 5 and re-read Ephesians 1:3-8 to be reassured of the rewards.

Matthew 7:13-14….tells us about the Narrow Gate as He speaks to me:

'Bob, You can enter God's Kingdom only through the narrow gate. The highway to hell is broad, and its gate is wide for the many who choose that way. But, Bob, the gateway to life is very narrow, and the road is difficult, and only a few ever find it.'

For a good response to that, go to Revelation 3:19-22. Let me share those verses with you also…

"I correct and discipline everyone I love, Bob. So be diligent and turn from your indifference."

'Look, Bob, I stand at the door and knock. If you hear my voice and open the door, (to your heart and life) I will come in, and we will share a meal (the word of God) together as friends. Those who are victorious will sit with me on my throne, just as I was victorious and sat with my Father on His throne.'

'Anyone with ears to hear, Bob, must listen to the Spirit and understand what He is saying to the churches.' And of course you know that we are those people of the churches.

<u>Reader response: Valuable information was gained for me. I have put a link to you on my site.</u>

Now, if you are an interested seeker, and wish to be made spiritually alive, let's learn the difference between a seeker, and a diligent seeker. For example, if you want spiritual ears to hear and spiritual eyes that see, you must first commit your life fully to Jesus for Him to use. (John 3:3) When you do, you will find a joy overwhelming while living for Him in this world. Let's look at what the bible says:

And now the prize awaits me—the crown of righteousness, which the Lord, the righteous Judge, will give me on the day of His return. And the prize is not just for me but for all who eagerly look forward to his appearing. **Timothy 4:8**

1 Corinthians 9:24-27 (New International Version - UK)

²⁴ Do you not know that in a race all the runners run, but only one gets the prize? Run in such a way as to get the prize.

²⁵ Everyone who competes in the games goes into strict training. They do it to get a crown that will not last; but we do it to get a crown that will last for ever.

²⁶ Therefore I do not run like a man running aimlessly; I do not fight like a man beating the air.

²⁷ No, I beat my body and make it my slave so that after I have preached to others, I myself will not be disqualified for the prize.

The Greatest Story Ever Told

Isaiah 49

This is one of the most precious chapters in the bible. We hear the voice of the Father commissioning His Son to bring about the spiritual rebirth of Israel, Then after their rejection, this salvation is offered to the Gentiles. We see the Messiah appointed by God as servant and Prince of God (Israel) in whom Jehovah would be glorified.

The Lord's Servant commissioned. (We hear the authoritative, incisive words of Jesus.)

Isaiah 49

The Servant of the LORD

[1] Listen to me, you islands; hear this, you distant nations: Before I was born the LORD called me; from my birth he has made mention of my name.

[2] He made my mouth like a sharpened sword, in the shadow of his hand he hid me; he made me into a polished arrow and concealed me in his quiver.

[3] He said to me, You are my servant, Israel, in whom I will display my splendor.

[4] But I said, I have labored to no purpose; I have spent my strength in vain and for nothing. Yet what is due to me is in the LORD'S hand, and my reward is with my God.

[5] And now the LORD says— he who formed me in the womb to be his servant to bring Jacob back to him and gather Israel to himself, for I am honored in the eyes of the LORD and my God has been my strength—

[6] He says: It is too small a thing for you to be my servant to restore the tribes of Jacob and bring back those of Israel I have kept. I will also make you a light for the Gentiles, that you may bring my salvation to the ends of the earth.

[7] This is what the LORD says— the Redeemer and Holy One of Israel— to him who was despised and abhorred by the nation, to the servant of rulers: Kings will see you and rise up,

princes will see and bow down, because of the LORD, who is faithful, the Holy One of Israel, who has chosen you.

Restoration of Israel

⁸ This is what the LORD says: In the time of my favor I will answer you, and in the day of salvation I will help you; I will keep you and will make you to be a covenant for the people, to restore the land and to reassign its desolate inheritances,

⁹ to say to the captives, 'Come out,' and to those in darkness, 'Be free!' They will feed beside the roads and find pasture on every barren hill.

¹⁰ They will neither hunger nor thirst, nor will the desert heat or the sun beat upon them. He who has compassion on them will guide them and lead them beside springs of water.

¹¹ I will turn all my mountains into roads, and my highways will be raised up.

¹² See, they will come from afar— some from the north, some from the west, some from the region of Aswan.

¹³Shout for joy, O heavens; rejoice, O earth; burst into song, O mountains! For the LORD comforts his people and will have compassion on his afflicted ones.

¹⁴But Zion said, The LORD has forsaken me, the Lord has forgotten me.

¹⁵Can a mother forget the baby at her breast and have no compassion on the child she has borne? Though she may forget, I will not forget you!

¹⁶ See, I have engraved you on the palms of my hands; your walls are ever before me.

¹⁷ Your sons hasten back, and those who laid you waste depart from you.

¹⁸ Lift up your eyes and look around; all your sons gather and come to you. As surely as I live, declares the LORD, you will wear them all as ornaments; you will put them on, like a bride.

¹⁹Though you were ruined and made desolate and your land laid waste, now you will be too small for your people, and those who devoured you will be far away.

²⁰ The children born during your bereavement will yet say in your hearing, 'This place is too small for us; give us more space to live in.'

²¹ Then you will say in your heart, 'Who bore me these? I was bereaved and barren; I was exiled and rejected. Who brought these up? I was left all alone, but these— where have they come from?'

²²This is what the Sovereign LORD says:

See, I will beckon to the Gentiles, I will lift up my banner to the peoples; they will bring your sons in their arms and carry your daughters on their shoulders.

²³ Kings will be your foster fathers, and their queens your nursing mothers. They will bow down before you with their faces to the ground; they will lick the dust at your feet. Then you will know that I am the LORD; those who hope in me will not be disappointed.

²⁴Can plunder be taken from warriors, or captives rescued from the fierce?

²⁵But this is what the LORD says: Yes, captives will be taken from warriors, and plunder retrieved from the fierce; I will contend with those who contend with you, and your children I will save.

²⁶ I will make your oppressors eat their own flesh; they will be drunk on their own blood, as with wine. Then all mankind will know that I, the LORD, am your Savior, your Redeemer, the Mighty One of Jacob

The Children of Abraham

John 8:31-32

³¹ To the Jews who had believed him, Jesus said, If you hold to my teaching, you are really my disciples. ³² Then you will know the truth, and the truth will set you free.

Put on the whole armor of God

Oh God Our Father, in Your Great Triune Glory!

Good Morning Almighty Father, Son and Holy Spirit.

Romans 12:1 indicates to me that I should speak these words to God: Today Heavenly Father, according to your Word I present my body a living sacrifice, Holy and acceptable in your sight. Then, Eph 6:12-19 follows with: Because I am not contending against flesh and blood, but against principalities, powers, world rulers of this present darkness and spiritual hosts of wickedness in the heavenly places, **I take the whole armor of God so that I may be able to stand in the evil day. So today I stand and gird my loins with truth. I put on the breastplate of righteousness. I shod my feet with the preparation of the gospel of peace. Above all these, I take the shield of salvation and the sword of the Spirit, which is the Word of God. I pray at all times in the Spirit with all my prayer and supplication for all God's family and for me that I may open my mouth boldly to proclaim the gospel. Then the weapons of my warfare are not worldly but have divine power to destroy strongholds. Today I destroy arguments and every proud obstacle to the knowledge of God and take every thought captive to obey Christ.**

Consider *Isaiah 58:8* with Thank you Father that according to your word the glory of the Lord is my rear guard. I praise you and thank you for the armor you have provided for me this day. I am completely covered now.

Because in Matt 16:18 it tells me that upon Jesus I have built my life. The gates of hell shall not prevail against me. Jesus, I apply your precious blood in my life, my family, my home and all my possessions. I declare to you the words of Psalms 23:1 'You are my shepherd and I shall not want.'

Phil. 4:13, 19 For you have supplied my needs according to your riches in glory. I can do all things through Christ who strengthens me.

We think about *1 Peter 5:6 for example:* Father, I humble myself under your mighty hand. I cast all my cares upon you as you care for me.

Psalms 103:3 exhorts the words of praise for you, because I am walking in divine health, for you Lord are my God who heals all my diseases. You tell me according to **Isaiah 53:5** that by your stripes I am healed. As in **3 John 1:2** I praise and thank you for my prosperity and good health even as my soul prospers. (Jesus is my life! And Hope.)

Jeremiah 1:12: Father, I have prayed according to your Word. You have said in your precious word that you would watch over it to perform it, as in **Proverbs 18:21, and** especially Proverbs 4:20-22,

Psalms 104:34 I am reminded that every word spoken becomes a living thing to minister life, or death and destruction. Lord Jesus, let my meditation be sweet to you as I will rejoice in you all day. Just rise up and live big within me. I am yours in the name of Jesus. Amen

To the church of the Thessalonians in God the Father and the Lord Jesus Christ: Grace and peace to you.

Grace and Peace to our readers as Well.

Thanksgiving for the Thessalonians' Faith

We always thank God for all of you, mentioning you in our prayers. We continually remember before our God and Father your work produced by faith, your labor prompted by love, and your endurance inspired by hope in our Lord Jesus Christ.

For we know, brothers loved by God, that he has chosen you, because our gospel came to you not simply with words, but also with power, with the Holy Spirit and with deep conviction. *You know how we lived among you for your sake.* You became imitators of us and of the Lord; in spite of severe suffering, *you welcomed the message with the joy given by the Holy Spirit.* And so you became a model to all the believers in Macedonia and Achaia. The Lord's message rang out from you not only in Macedonia and Achaia—your faith in God has become known everywhere. Therefore we do not need to say anything about it, for they themselves report what kind of reception you gave us. They tell how you turned to God from idols to serve the living and true God, and to wait for his Son from heaven, whom he raised from the dead— Jesus, who rescues us from the coming wrath. **1 Thessalonians 1:1-10**

Ephesians 6:14-19 (New International Reader's Version)

14 So stand firm. Put the belt of truth around your waist. Put the armor of godliness on your chest. 15 Wear on your feet what will prepare you to tell the good news of peace. 16 Also, pick up the shield of faith. With it you can put out all of the flaming arrows of the evil one. 17 Put on the helmet of salvation. And take the sword of the Holy Spirit. The sword is God's word.

18 At all times, pray by the power of the Spirit. Pray all kinds of prayers. Be watchful, so that you can pray. Always keep on praying for all of God's people.

19 Pray also for me. Pray that when I open my mouth, the right words will be given to me. Then I can be bold as I tell the mystery of the good news.

Enjoy these foundational verses to help you in your personal relationship with Jesus Christ:

I have written this to you who believe in the name of the Son of God, so that you may know you have eternal life. **1 John 5:13** And we are confident that He hears us whenever we ask for anything that pleases Him. And since we know He hears us when we make our requests, we also know that He will give us what we ask for.

We know that those who are children of God do not keep on sinning. The Son of God keeps them safe. The evil one can't harm them.

We know that we are children of God. We know that the whole world is under the control of the evil one. **1 John 5:18-19**

We accept the witness of people. But the witness of God is more important because it is God who gives it. He has given witness about his Son. Those who believe in the Son of God have accepted that witness in their hearts. Those who do not believe God's witness are calling him a liar. That's because they have not believed his witness about his Son. **1 John 5:9-10**

Jesus Christ is the one who was baptized in water and died on the cross. He wasn't just baptized in water. He also died on the cross.

The Holy Spirit has given a truthful witness about him. That's because the Spirit is the truth. **1 John 5:6**

Following God Is No Accident. Obeying Him Is A Calling.

Leviticus 23:3.....The seventh day is God's day of rest.

Psalm 24.....Who is the Lord? He is the King of Glory.

Acts 21.....In the uproar of the crowd Paul was ready to die.....

After having been warned not to go to Jerusalem.

Walk close to Jesus.....Wise leadership is crucial.

Malachi 2:7.....A Priest should be trustworthy, because many people seek instructions from his mouth.

Insights from God Almighty.

The Final Judgment

And I saw a great white throne and the one sitting on it. The earth and sky fled from his presence, but they found no place to hide. I saw the dead, both great and small, standing before God's throne. And the books were opened, including the Book of Life. And the dead were judged according to what they had done, as recorded in the books. The sea gave up its dead, and death and the grave gave up their dead. And all were judged according to their deeds. Then death and the grave were thrown into the lake of fire. This lake of fire is the second death. And anyone whose name was not found recorded in the Book of Life was thrown into the lake of fire. **Revelation 20:11-15**

The Spirit and the bride say, "Come." Let anyone who hears this say, "Come." Let anyone who is thirsty come. Let anyone who desires, drink freely from the water of life. **Revelation 22:17**

As you begin with chapter one (1) of "A Chosen Life Study", you will appreciate looking back on these powerful verses to stay abreast of the Holy Spirit's work in your life; then continue on with the zeal He provides you with. **Please continue your search for God through the body and blood of Jesus Christ.**

Jesus told him, "I am the way, the truth, and the life. No one can come to the Father except through me." **John 14:6**

Quite naturally, even without saying, the dove in this book represents the Holy Spirit.

Jesus sent Him to enable us to understand, and to make the 'Elect Holy.' He calls us to announce in our hearts the words 'Abba Father.' He is also responsible and illuminates each page of this book.

Luke 11:13 (New International Version)

[13]"If you then, though you are evil, know how to give good gifts to your children, how much more will your Father in heaven give the Holy Spirit to those who ask him!"

Bob, Your book is like a teaching manual. Chapters are set up to be studied. It is not read like a novel, so each chapter must be absorbed, reviewed and re-read again, It does not need editing, it is virtually error free.

Signed,

Buddy Dow

Publishing Consultant

Author House

Chapter One

A Chosen Life Study

Our Cornerstone of Faith

As we incline our hearts and minds to the knowledge of Our

Wonderful Counselor

Mighty God Everlasting Father

Prince of Peace. Isaiah 9:6

His Church

Our life in The Cornerstone, while being changed from glory to glory in and with Jesus, is connected to one another in Him. It maintains a deep relationship with Jesus and His church. Waverly Open Bible emulates for our family the Word of God, and it keeps us flowing in Him. It is a church in Christ that truly has opened their bible to His love, and His ways. We are rooted and built up in Him, **(Col. 2:7)** steadfast in the faith that only Jesus can provide. And with that we have committed our lives to establish a personal relationship with Jesus Christ on an individual basis. The basic truth with that is loving Him as we reach out to one another in love while sharing His Word, and our lives. It is overflowing, as we partner with Him and with one another.

Knowing who we are is the basis for the above statements, and is the resounding format of Christianity.

You were dead because of your sins and because *your sinful nature was not yet cut away.* Then God made you alive with Christ, for He forgave all our sins.

He canceled the record of the charges against us and took it away by nailing it to the cross. In this way, He disarmed the spiritual rulers and authorities. He shamed them publicly by His victory over them on the cross. (You must receive Christ.)

Colossians 2:13-15

The basics for understanding this chapter, and book, is knowing what it means to be embodied in Christ, and with that, having been immersed in Him?

So, what is immersion?

For example, in just 5 months my wife and I will have been married for 50 years. Yet I cannot say that all of the time I have been immersed in her, or with her. Yet I have the best wife and mother anyone could want. She sometimes complains about a lack of my attention. The commandments teach us to put nothing ahead of God. He is first in all our ways.

So how can we make Him always first in our lives? Is that a possibility? God says in John 3:3 that we need to be born again. Could it be that He would come into our life and be immersed with us in His Spirit, if only we would ask? Well as we read this book, let's see if Jesus is the God of our ways, and that He fills our days and nights with His presence, our need, and with His desire to create a better life for us, if only we ask. How do we make that happen? Flow through this chapter with the dove, and let Him explain the first step. It's like a song that expresses the words, 'Oh how He loves you and me', then let's ask ourselves if we are always connected in Him? Pray! Be faithfully positive, be honest, and surely be long serving in your mind and in your heart with God in the Lord Jesus Christ.

God is building His church through His Son.

Jeremiah 31:31-33 *"The day is coming,' says the Lord, when I will make a new covenant with the people of Israel and Judah. This covenant will not be like the one I made with their ancestors when I took them by the hand and brought them out of the land of Egypt. They broke that covenant, though I loved them as a husband loves his wife," says the Lord. "But this is the new covenant I will make with the people of Israel on that day," says the Lord.*

Do you really want to be saved? Do you know we are all sinners? Are you ready to confess your sinfulness and lead a pure life, accepting the Lord Jesus Christ as payment for your sinfulness? Open, to Jesus and others? It will be answered lovingly in **John 3:3-10**.....Please read! It is possible, through His Holy Spirit which He offers freely. In **John 3:3-10** notice how completely helpless the cripple man was to be cleansed and to be healed, by the water and the word. He had a longing for God's Kingdom. What does Jesus want to do with us as we continue reading below? Needless to say, but, the words below are *very important! We also build confidence as His Spirit leads us.*

"I will put my instructions deep within them, and I will write them on their hearts. I will be their God, and they will be my people. They will not need to teach their neighbors, nor will they need to teach their relatives, saying, 'You should know the Lord.' For everyone, from the least to the greatest, will know me already," says the Lord. "And I will forgive their wickedness, and I will never again remember their sins."

In **1 John**, **3 Verse 1,** we read: See how very much our Father loves us, for he calls us His children, and that is what we are! But the people who belong to this world don't recognize that we are God's children because they don't know him.

Verse 2: Dear friends, we are already God's children, but He has not yet shown us what we will be like when Christ appears. But we do know that we will be like Him, for we will see Him as he really is. And all who have this eager expectation will keep themselves pure, just as He is pure.

Verse 4: Everyone who sins is breaking God's law, for all sin is contrary to the law of God. *And you know that Jesus came to take away our sins, and there is no sin in Him.*

Anyone who continues to live in Him will not sin. But anyone who keeps on sinning does not know Him, or understand who He is.

Verse 7: Dear children, don't let anyone deceive you about this: When people do what is right, it shows that they are righteous, even as Christ is righteous. But when people keep on sinning, it shows that they belong to the devil, who has been sinning since the world's beginning. But the Son of God came to destroy the works of the devil.

Those who have been born into God's family do not make a practice of sinning, because God's life is in them. (Born again) So they can't keep on sinning, because they are children of God.

Verse 10: So now we can tell who are children of God and who are children of the devil. Anyone who does not live righteously and does not love other believers does not belong to God.

1 John 1-10

I, Bob, included these verses because they are so outstanding and wonderful to read. If His joy doesn't fill us each day of our lives, we should reread these verses every day of our lives.

God is building His church, and He is using His Son to do that.

When He opened His door for me, why did He give me a choice to enter, or to choose my own love song, and enter in my own time? 'This mystery' is for believers only. Others have yet to discover what is on the inside.

Hosea's wife is redeemed as God redeems His children

Then the Lord said to me, "Go and love your wife again, even though she commits adultery with another lover. This will illustrate that the Lord still loves Israel, even though the people have turned to other gods and love to worship them."

 How do we forgive a grievous sin? Our Lord has given us that grace!

So I bought her back for fifteen pieces of silver and five bushels of barley and a measure of wine. (Evangelism begins here:) (I hear His voice through Hosea---command of the Lord fulfilling. In denouncing sin, we lead others to Jesus.)

Then I said to her, "You must live in my house for many days and stop your prostitution. During this time, you will not have sexual relations with anyone, not even with me."

This shows that Israel will go a long time without a king or prince, and without sacrifices, sacred pillars, priests, or even idols!

But afterward the people will return and devote themselves to the Lord their God and to David's descendant, their king. In the last days, they will tremble in awe of the Lord and of his goodness. Hosea 3:1-5

Knowing who we are is the basis of Christianity

Christians know and love one another by the power in His name

And the truth about our fellowship adds glory to His fame.

It will always be a mystery, how He draws His precious ones

To believe and trust in Jesus, while He calls us all His sons.

He says it's like the wind that blows; we feel it when it nears,

But can't tell where it comes from, or where it disappears.

The one thing that believers know: A change has taken place,

As our hearts have entered into the witness of His grace.

And so we know each other and praise our Lord above,

For the earthly view of paradise, in the comfort of His love…

Believe His Holy name, all you children of the Lord,

Don't go anywhere with out Him, He's our shield and so adored…

 Poem By Bob Bowman

Flowing Through Ephesians Chapter Three

For this reason because I preached that you are thus built up together, I, Paul, [am] the prisoner of Jesus the Christ for the sake and on behalf of you Gentiles.

Assuming that you have heard of the stewardship of God's grace (His unmerited favor) that was entrusted to me [to dispense to you] for your benefit,

[And] that the mystery (secret) was made known to me and I was allowed to comprehend it by direct revelation, as I already briefly wrote you.

When you read this you can understand my insight into the mystery of Christ.

[This mystery] was never disclosed to human beings in past generations as it has now been revealed to His holy apostles (consecrated messengers) and prophets by the [Holy] Spirit.

[It is this:] that the Gentiles are now to be fellow heirs [with the Jews], members of the same body and joint partakers [sharing] in the same divine promise in Christ through [their acceptance of] the glad tidings (the Gospel). Of this [Gospel] I was made a minister according to the gift of God's free grace (undeserved favor) which was bestowed on me by the exercise (the working in all its effectiveness) of His power.

To me, though I am the very least of all the saints (God's consecrated people), this grace (favor, privilege) was granted and graciously entrusted: to proclaim to the Gentiles the unending (boundless, fathomless, incalculable, and exhaustless) riches of Christ [wealth which no human being could have searched out],

Also to enlighten all men and make plain to them what is the plan [regarding the Gentiles and providing for the salvation of all men] of the mystery kept hidden through the ages and concealed until now in [the mind of] God Who created all things by Christ Jesus. [The purpose is] that through the church the [c]complicated, many-sided wisdom of God in all its infinite variety and innumerable aspects might now be made known to the angelic rulers and authorities (principalities and powers) in the heavenly sphere.

This is in accordance with the terms of the eternal and timeless purpose which He has realized and carried into effect in [the person of] Christ Jesus our Lord,

In Whom, because of our faith in Him, we dare to have the boldness (courage and confidence) of free access (an unreserved approach to God with freedom and without fear).

So I ask you not to lose heart [not to faint or become despondent through fear] at what I am suffering in your behalf. [Rather glory in it] for it is an honor to you.

For this reason [[d]seeing the greatness of this plan by which you are built together in Christ], I bow my knees before the Father of our Lord Jesus Christ,

For Whom every family in heaven and on earth is named [that Father from Whom all fatherhood takes its title and derives its name].

May He grant you out of the rich treasury of His glory to be strengthened and reinforced with mighty power in the inner man by the [Holy] Spirit [Himself indwelling your innermost being and personality].

May Christ through your faith [actually] dwell (settle down, abide, make His permanent home) in your hearts! May you be rooted deep in love and founded securely on love,

That you may have the power and be strong to apprehend and grasp with all the saints [God's devoted people, the experience of that love] what is the breadth and length and height and depth [of it];

[That you may really come] to know [practically, [e]through experience for yourselves] the love of Christ, which far surpasses [f]mere knowledge [without experience]; that you may be filled [through all your being] [g]unto all the fullness of God [may have the richest measure of the divine Presence, and [h]become a body wholly filled and flooded with God Himself]!

Now to Him Who, by (in consequence of) the [action of His] power that is at work within us, is able to [carry out His purpose and] do superabundantly, far over and above all that we [dare] ask or think [infinitely beyond our highest prayers, desires, thoughts, hopes, or dreams]--

To Him be glory in the church and in Christ Jesus throughout all generations forever and ever. Amen (so be it). Ephesians Chapter three Ending

Prayer

God answers all prayers

He hears us, loves us, and desires to live with us.

Because He wants to protect us He uses His will to protect ours.

So, when we pray, He deals with the issue more than how it is presented or requested…(His will not ours) That's why we don't always understand why He didn't answer our prayer.

I Share these many verses with you, because like meat and potatoes build your physical body, so God's undefiled word will build your spiritual body. In other words, ***getting ready to meet our Savior.***

Conclusion: Always pray without ceasing!

This is what our Faithful Lord ***who cannot lie*** has declared to me!

If you abide in Me, and my Words abide in you, you will ask what you desire, and it shall be done for you. **John 15:7**

Therefore, I say to you, whatever things you ask when you pray, believe that you receive them, and you will have them. **Mark 11:24**

And whatever things you ask in prayer, believing, you will receive.

 Matthew 21:22

And whatever you ask in My name, that I will do, that the Father may be glorified in the Son. If you ask anything in My name, I will do it. **John 14:13-14**

Again I say to you that if two of you agree concerning anything that they ask, it will be done for them by My Father in heaven. **Matthew 18:19**

Ask, and it will be given unto you; seek, and you will find; knock and it will be opened unto you. For everyone who asks receives, and he who seeks finds, and to him who knocks it will be opened. **Matthew. 7:7,8**

And shall God not avenge His own elect who cry out day and night to Him, though He bears long with them. I tell you that He will avenge them speedily. **Luke 18:7,8**

The effective, fervent prayer of a righteous man avails much. **James 5:16**

Now this is the confidence that we have in Him, that if we ask anything according to His will, He hears us. And if we know that He hears us, whatever we ask, we know that we have the petitions that we have asked of Him. 1 **John 5:14-15**

Does God really want us to be His? Called by His name? To be a shining light? Do my ways reflect His? Do I always abide with Him….. Is my prayer life in obedience to my walk with the Lord?

When I answer a questions within myself regarding the suggested thoughts above, and verses above I always refer to the Statement of Jesus that He allowed us to build our faith with in **2 Corinthians 13:5** as follows: Examine yourselves to see if your faith is genuine. Test yourselves. Surely you know that Jesus Christ is living in you; if not, you have failed the test of genuine faith. As you test yourselves, I hope you will recognize that we have not failed the test of apostolic authority.

Do I hold to this thought in my heart? To be sure!

For everyone has sinned! We all fall short of God's glorious standard. Yet God, with undeserved kindness, declares that we are righteous. **Roman's 3:23-24**

Can Jesus forgive our sins if He hasn't been invited into our heart and become our personal Savior? Like a friend that is better than a brother? Is your relationship with Him personal, and does it bother you to sin? Does your human nature convince you, and does your heart commit you to Him? Would you be lonely without Him?

1 John 1

The Word of Life

Here is what we announce to everyone about the Word of life. This life was present and He was already here from the beginning. We have heard him. We have seen him with our eyes. We have looked at him. Our hands have touched him.

That life has appeared. We have seen him. We give witness about him. And we announce to you that same eternal life. He was already with the Father. He has appeared to us.

We announce to you what we have seen and heard. We do it so you can share life together with us. And we share life with the Father and with His Son, Jesus Christ.

We are writing this to make our joy complete. **Verses one through four.**

Walking in the Light

Here is the message we have heard from him and announce to you. God is light.

There is no darkness in him at all.

Suppose we say that we share life with God but still walk in the darkness. Then

we are lying. We are not living by the truth. But suppose we walk in the light, just as he is in the light. Then we share life with one another. And the blood of Jesus, his Son, makes us pure from all sin.

Suppose we claim we are without sin. Then we are fooling ourselves. The truth is

not in us.

But God is faithful and fair. If we admit that we have sinned, he will forgive us our

sins. He will forgive every wrong thing we have done. He will make us pure.

If we say we have not sinned, we are calling God a liar. His word has no place in.

our lives. **Verses five through ten.**

I Would be True
Howard A. Walter 1883-1918 Joseph
Yates Peek 1843-1911

1. I would be true, for there are those who trust me; I would be pure, for there are those who care. I would be strong, for there is much to suffer; I would be brave, for there is much to dare—I would be brave, for there is much to dare.

2. I would be friend of all—the foe, the friend–less; I would be giving, and for–get the gift. I would be hum–ble, for I know my weakness; I would look up, and laugh, and love, and lift—I would look up, and laugh, and love, and lift.

3. I would be prayerful thru each bus–y moment; I would be constantly in touch with God. I would be tuned to hear his slightest whisper; I would have faith to keep the path Christ trod--I would have faith to keep the path Christ trod.

Unless the Lord builds a house, the work of the builders is wasted.

Unless the Lord protects a city, Guarding it with sentries will do no good.

Psalm 127:1

And this is what God has testified: He has given us eternal life, and this life is in His Son. *Whoever has the Son has life*; whoever does not have God's Son does not have life. **John 5:11-12**

Sometimes our human mind won't listen, or try to understand the message of love from God, or attempt to learn of the love He has for them.

But Moses protested again, "What if they won't believe me or listen to me? What if they say: 'The Lord never appeared to you'?" **Exodus 4:1**

Do as He tells us and we will never be sorry in the long haul.

Now go! I will be with you as you speak, and I will instruct you in what to say."

Exodus 1:12

The King adopts an orphan

Worship from the Heart

"Father, I'm speechless when I read that I am Your child. You have lavished on me the love due a King's son with all it implies. When the reality of Your claim on my life doesn't sink in and I'm wandering the dark alleys looking for scraps, bring me back to the realization of who I am in You."

Walk Thru the Word

New Testament: 1 John 3:1-10

Old Testament: Hosea 3:1-5

WEDNESDAY AUGUST 22

Behold what manner of love the Father has bestowed on us, that we should be called children of God! (1 John 3:1).

One father, when asked about his feelings for his son, responded, "Of course I love him; he's my son!"

Another man, who had an adopted son, was asked the same question. He replied, "Of course he's my son; see how I love him!"

Which father's love would you rather have?

In John's letter, the apostle proclaims the greatness of the Father's love because He has adopted wayward men and women into His family. Reflect on the privilege of becoming one of God's children as you read Albert Barnes' exposition.

Walk with Albert Barnes

"There is no higher love that can be shown than in adopting a poor and friendless orphan, and giving him a parent and a home. Even God could bestow upon us no more valuable token of affection than that we should be adopted into His family, and permitted to regard Him as our Father.

"When we remember how insignificant we are as creatures, and how ungrateful, rebellious, and vile we have been as sinners, we may well be amazed at the love which would adopt us into the holy family of God so that we may be treated as the children of the Most High.

"A prince could manifest no higher love for a wandering, ragged, vicious orphan boy found in the streets than by adopting him into his own family, and admitting him to the same privileges as his own sons; and yet this would be a trifle compared with the honor which God has bestowed on us."

Walk Closer to God

Do you, like Jesus, carry out your Father's commands not to earn His love, but to acknowledge it? Notice John's desires for his spiritual children— that they do not keep on sinning, nor let themselves be led astray.

Walk in obedience to God and in harmony with other believers. It's one good way to tell the world— without saying a word—"Of course God is my Father; see how He loves me!"

This Devotion is used with the permission of Walk through the Bible. It was used by them in their August 22, 07 issue

God's Sovereign Choice

God's selection of Israel with Christ as my witness, I speak with utter truthfulness. My conscience and the Holy Spirit confirm it. My heart is filled with bitter sorrow and unending grief for my people, my Jewish brothers and sisters. I would be willing to be forever cursed—cut off from Christ!—if that would save them. They are the people of Israel, chosen to be God's adopted children. God revealed His glory to them. He made covenants with them and gave them His law. He gave them the privilege of worshiping Him and receiving His wonderful promises. Abraham, Isaac, and Jacob are their ancestors, and Christ himself was an Israelite as far as His human nature is concerned. And He is God, the one who rules over everything and is worthy of eternal praise! Amen.

Well then, has God failed to fulfill his promise to Israel? No, for not all who are born into the nation of Israel are truly members of God's people! Being descendants of Abraham doesn't make them truly Abraham's children. For the Scriptures say, "Isaac is the son through whom your descendants will be counted," though Abraham had other children, too. This means that Abraham's physical descendants are not necessarily children of God. Only the children of the promise are considered to be Abraham's children. For God had promised, "I will return about this time next year, and Sarah will have a son."

This son was our ancestor Isaac. When he married Rebecca, she gave birth to twins. But before they were born, before they had done anything good or bad, she received a message from God. (This message shows that God chooses people according to His own purposes; He calls people, but not according to their good or bad works.) She was told, "Your older son will serve your younger son." In the words of the Scriptures, "I loved Jacob, but I rejected Esau."

Are we saying, then, that God was unfair? Of course not! For God said to Moses,

"I will show mercy to anyone I choose, and I will show compassion to anyone I choose."

So it is God who decides to show mercy. We can neither choose it nor work for it.

For the Scriptures say that God told Pharaoh, "I have appointed you for the very purpose of displaying my power in you and to spread my fame throughout the earth." So you see, God chooses to show mercy to some, and He chooses to harden the hearts of others so they refuse to listen.

Well then, you might say, "Why does God blame people for not responding? Haven't they simply done what He makes them do?"

No, don't say that. Who are you, a mere human being, to argue with God? Should the thing that was created say to the one who created it, "Why have you made me like this?" When a potter makes jars out of clay, doesn't he have a right to use the same lump of clay to make one jar for decoration and another to throw garbage into? In the same way, even though God has the right to show His anger and His power, He is very patient with those on whom His anger falls, who are destined for destruction. He does this to make the riches of His glory shine even brighter on those to whom He shows mercy, who were prepared in advance for glory. And we are among those whom He selected, both from the Jews and from the Gentiles.

Concerning the Gentiles, God says in the prophecy of Hosea.

"Those who were not my people, I will now call my people. And I will love those whom I did not love before." And, "Then, at the place where they were told, 'You are not my people,' there they will be called 'children of the living God.'" And concerning Israel, Isaiah the prophet cried out,

"Though the people of Israel are as numerous as the sand of the seashore, only a remnant will be saved. For the LORD will carry out His sentence upon the earth quickly and with finality." And Isaiah said the same thing in another place: "If the LORD of Heaven's Armies had not spared a few of our children, we would have been wiped out like Sodom, destroyed like Gomorrah." **Romans 9:1-29**

Israel's Unbelief.

What does all this mean? Even though the Gentiles were not trying to follow God's standards, they were made right with God. And it was by faith that this took place. But the people of Israel, who tried so hard to get right with God by keeping the law, never succeeded. Why not? Because they were trying to get right with God by keeping the law instead of by trusting in Him. They stumbled over the great rock in their path. God warned them of this in the Scriptures when He said,

"I am placing a stone in Jerusalem that makes people stumble, a rock that makes them fall. But anyone who trusts in Him will never be disgraced." Romans 9:30-33

If you never met me, you have missed nothing...." But, If you have not met Jesus Christ you are not enjoying a personal relationship, or understanding that your sins are forgiven through His shed- blood. In reality, your sins have not been nailed to the cross with Jesus, and you have missed everything.

Christ is the strength of our lives, and forever God has used His ways to prove that to us. The article above of Israel is His example of that to us.

Reaching for His Righteousness...With A Light From The Son

Please Read and write your own comments for **John 14:1-6**... A Very Important thought provoking text not to be taken lightly.

'Believers Should Stand Firm'

As for us, we can't help but thank God for you, dear brothers and sisters loved by the Lord. We are always thankful that God chose you to be among the first to experience salvation—a salvation that came through the Spirit who makes you holy and through your belief in the truth. He called you to salvation when we told you the Good News; now you can share in the glory of our Lord Jesus Christ. **2 Thessalonians 2:13**

Most likely we have never met, nor have we been invited together to a greater event in this life than the one we are undertaking to read now...

Let me reveal to you the wonderful Good News of the gospel.

'The Resurrected Body'

In Jesus we have a bond. Yesterday, Today and forever.

But someone may ask, 'How will the dead be raised? What kind of bodies will they have?' What a foolish question! When you put a seed into the ground, it doesn't grow into a plant unless it dies first. And what you put in the ground is not the plant that will grow, but only a bare seed of wheat or whatever you are planting. Then God gives it the new body he wants it to have. A different plant grows from each kind of seed. Similarly there are different kinds of flesh—one kind for humans, another for animals, another for birds, and another for fish.

There are also bodies in the heavens and bodies on the earth. The glory of the heavenly bodies is different from the glory of the earthly bodies. The sun has one kind of glory, while the moon and stars each have another kind. And even the stars differ from each other in their glory.

It is the same way with the resurrection of the dead. Our earthly bodies are planted in the ground when we die, but they will be raised to live forever. Our bodies are buried in brokenness, but they will be raised in glory. They are buried in weakness, but they will be raised in strength. They are buried as natural human bodies, but they will be raised as spiritual bodies. For just as there are natural bodies, there are also spiritual bodies.

The Scriptures tell us, "The first man, Adam, became a living person. But the last Adam—that is, Christ—is a life-giving Spirit. What comes first is the natural body, then the spiritual body comes later. Adam, the first man, was made from the dust of the earth, while Christ, the second man, came from heaven. Earthly people are like the earthly man, and heavenly people are like the heavenly man. Just as we are now like the earthly man, we will someday be like the heavenly man."

What I am saying, dear brothers and sisters, is that our physical bodies cannot inherit the Kingdom of God. These dying bodies cannot inherit that which will last forever.

But let me reveal to you a wonderful secret. We will not all die, but we will all be transformed! It will happen in a moment, in the blink of an eye, when the last trumpet is blown. For when the trumpet sounds, those who have died will be raised to live forever. And we who are living will also be transformed. For our dying bodies must be transformed into bodies that will never die; our mortal bodies must be transformed into immortal bodies. Then, when our dying bodies have been transformed into bodies that will never die, this Scripture will be fulfilled:

"Death is swallowed up in victory.

Death where is your victory?
O death, where is your sting?"

For sin is the sting that results in death, and the law gives sin its power. But thank God! He gives us victory over sin and death through our Lord Jesus Christ.

So, my dear brothers and sisters, be strong and immovable. Always work enthusiastically for the Lord, for you know that nothing you do for the Lord is ever useless. **1 Corinthians 15:35-58**

We are never alone, my friend. By His power we live every minute and second in the truth about Jesus, today, tomorrow & forever. He plants it there! Thy will be done. His Spirit must be in charge, and you must ask for Him with a zeal of contentment. Just put Him first. Lift Him up in daily bible reading, and praise Him.

Psalm 23

New Living Translation (**NLT**)

Holy Bible. New Living Translation copyright © 1996, 2004 by Tyndale Charitable Trust

Used by permission of Tyndale House Publishers.

The 23ʳᵈ Psalm

A psalm of David:

The Lord is my shepherd;
I have all that I need.
He lets me rest in green meadows;
he leads me beside peaceful streams.
He renews my strength.
He guides me along right paths,
bringing honor to his name.
(Even when I walk
through the darkest valley,
I will not be afraid,
for you are close beside me.)
Your rod and your staff

protect and comfort me.
You prepare a feast for me
in the presence of my enemies.
You honor me by anointing my head with oil.
My cup overflows with blessings.
Surely your goodness and unfailing love will pursue me
all the days of my life,
and I will live in the house of the Lord
forever.

A Life That Lives By His Plan And Purposes

"The thief's purpose is to steal and kill and destroy. My purpose is to give life in all its fullness."**John 10:10...**

I want to love you like He did, 'by sharing His truth.'

We learn and understand that the spiritual life God has given to us is actually the most important part of us. In my earlier days, the most important part of my life was my physical life (as opposed to my spiritual life), and it demanded me to compete and to be superior in whatever I undertook to do. With me, it was a very short-lived assessment, and I quickly learned what was within my grasp and what was beyond it.

Most people were better "equipped" than I was, but I wondered where their talents would take them. Athletically, many were overachievers and gifted with great success. It seemed many were intellectually bound for the higher things in life. Although my brain seemed adequate, I never wanted all of it to be exposed at once. So my thought process lingered to the outer limits of my understanding, then it would return in the form of contentment—I am what I am, and I seemed to understand that it was all from God. I felt He loved me for understanding that part of me, as well as loving Him for His presence in my life. But how does God relate to my contentment? Did He want me, with the equipment that He had gifted me with, to become someone that no one else was? And most importantly, did I understand His gifts and how to use them? I understood the first gift to be considered was the gift of love. I have never found anyone in my travels that doesn't need it, and most recognize their need for it. God has gifted many with the wonderful gift of music, which is a real blessing to all of us. He gifted me with turning wonderful words of praise to Him into a form of poems that are meant to glorify our Lord, as well as being a source of fellowshipping with other believers.

A large part of the desire that caused me to write A Chosen Life Study came from the gift of writing poems. First and foremost, however, was the never-ending passion to have people everywhere know and trust the Lord Jesus Christ. To be able to praise Him for who He is, as well as to gain the salvation that He had died to give us.

Well, of all the things that I would have lost; being without Jesus forever would have been the worst. It would have also been the most impossible one to endure. To be lost without Christ, and His salvation! Dear me, what could be worse.

What in this life has brought you the real joy of living, that will last you forever? Filling you with an awesome sense of belonging to the God of all love and mercy, the God of all ages?. Well, that is what I found in His word with Jesus. He is the anchor for my soul, and there is nothing in all this world, or the next that can sustain me without Him and His Word that testifies about Him, and His love for everyone. His blood is a covenant that can never-ever be surpassed, or diminished.

Reaching For His Righteousness..... In the Light of His Son

From His abundance we have all received one gracious blessing after another, through the Prophetic Word Of God. For the law was given through Moses, but God's unfailing love and faithfulness came through Jesus Christ. No one has ever seen God. But the unique One, who is Himself God, and is near to the Father's heart. He has revealed God to us. Testifying to **John 1:16-17**

For out of His fullness (abundance) we have all received [all had a share and we were all supplied with] one grace after another and spiritual blessing upon spiritual blessing and even favor upon favor and gift [heaped] upon gift. Thank you, Blessed Father!

John 1:16-17..... Write your hopes, your dreams, your prayers in spaces where room permits. Where the Spirit convinces you.

What is God's fullest blessing to you that caused you to praise and adore Him?

What caused you to follow Him closer? Was it to find fellowship with other believers?...Or, was it when you found out that you couldn't always keep His commands. Then what Jesus has done for us, and that He was first and foremost. Moses gave us the law; But Jesus Christ gave us Grace and Truth

Do you remember your first bible class? How about the first verses He shared with you? Where are some of those members? Do you still pray for them?

The Bible is God's Own Revealed Word to us.

The unbeliever thinks and believes that the prophets wrote the Bible. Instead of it being God-breathed; he thinks man's thoughts enter into the substance. **In 2 Peter 1:20-21** God didn't need man to write the Bible, but to all who believe that it is inspired, and written by Himself, To them He gave the right to become children of God. Still, man can't believe on his own, even when the handwriting is on the wall; as told by the Prophet Daniel; below:

This Life in the Spirit reveals this story in Daniel: Suddenly the fingers of a human hand appeared and wrote on the plaster of the wall near the lamp stand in the royal palace. The king watched the hand as it wrote. His face turned pale and he was so frightened that his knees knocked together and his legs gave way. LOL The king called out for the enchanter, astrologers and diviners to be brought and said to these wise men of Babylon, "Whoever reads this writing and tells me what it means will be clothed in purple and have a gold chain around his neck, and will be made the third highest ruler in the kingdom." *Daniel 5:5–7*

So Daniel was brought before the king, and the king said to him, "Are you Daniel, one of the exiles my father the king brought to Judah? I have heard that the spirit of the gods is in you and that you have insight, intelligence and outstanding wisdom. The wise men and enchanters were brought before me to read this writing and tell me what it means, but they could not explain it. Now I have heard that you are able to give interpretations and to solve difficult problems.

If you can read this writing and tell me what it means, you will be clothed in purple and have a gold chain placed around your neck, and you will be made the third highest ruler in the kingdom." Then Daniel answered the king, "You may keep your gifts for yourself and give your rewards to someone else. Nevertheless, I will read the writing for the king and tell him what it means**." *Daniel 5:13–17*

Daniel isn't here to interpret the Bible for us today, but the Holy Spirit is, and every believer praises God for His presence. There is only one thing in this life that is more important than trusting the Bible; that is using the Bible and seeking its blessings through its promises. Sweet corn can't grow unless it is fed and watered. The use of His word waters us. His word brings roots. His soil makes us grow. **1 Peter 2:2**.....Learn what rocks have to do with all of this. But you were purchased with the *precious blood of Christ, the Messiah,* like that of a sacrificial lamb without blemish or spot. It is true that He was chosen and foreknown for this before the foundation of the world, but He was brought out to the public view and made manifest in these last days for your sake.

Through Him you believe in and rely on God who raised Him up from the dead and gave Him honor and glory, so that your faith and hope are centered and rested in God.

Since by your obedience to the Truth through the Holy Spirit you have purified your hearts for the sincere affection of the brethren, see that you love one another fervently from a pure heart.

You have been regenerated, born again, not from a mortal origin seed, sperm, but from one that is immortal by the ever living and lasting Word of God. For all flesh mankind is like grass, and all its glory honor

like the flower of grass. The grass withers and the flower drops off,

But the Word of the Lord divine instruction, the Gospel) endures forever. And this Word is the good news which was preached to you. *1 Peter 1:19–25*

Treasure in Fragile Clay Jars

(Looking at **Jude verse 22** we find that people who believe in God, but lack the discipline of total commitment may even live as an abomination to the Spirit. So, from my own understanding I have used the veil in the box here that we may love one another enough to warn them about what scripture is saying. Sin makes salvation fragile for us, but our lives and those of others are worth watching out for....'**I only know that Jesus died, and that He died for me.' You too!**)

2 Corinthians 4

Therefore, since God in his mercy has given us this 'New way,' we never give up. We reject all shameful deeds and underhanded methods. We don't try to trick anyone or distort the word of God. We tell the truth before God, and all who are honest know this.

If the Good News we preach is hidden behind a veil, it is hidden only from people who are perishing. (The bible say's that it is not God's intention that any person should perish.) Find out why some are perishing; and pull them from the fires of hell as told to us in verse **22 of the book of Jude.** Refute [so as to] convict some who dispute with you; and on some have mercy who waver and doubt. I am being careful of what I say, I have blended my thoughts with scripture to face the truth. Satan, who is the god of this world, has blinded the minds of those who don't believe. They are unable to see the glorious light of the Good News. They don't understand this message about the glory of Christ, who is the exact likeness of God. And in doing so they have rejected the gift of God in Christ Jesus which brings eternal life. Can you imagine or believe.....Never dying! And the next face you see when you leave here will be Jesus. Are you thirsty?

You see, we don't go around preaching about ourselves. We preach that Jesus Christ is Lord, and we ourselves are your servants for Jesus' sake. For God, who said, "Let there be light in the darkness," has made this light shine in our hearts so we could know the glory of God that is seen in the face of Jesus Christ.

We now have this light shining in our hearts, but we ourselves are like fragile clay jars containing this great treasure. This makes it clear that our great power is from God, not from ourselves.

We are pressed on every side by troubles, but we are not crushed. We are perplexed, but not driven to despair. We are hunted down, but never abandoned by God. We get knocked down, but we are not destroyed. Through suffering, our bodies continue to share in the death of Jesus so that the life of Jesus may also be seen in our bodies.

Yes, we live under constant danger of death because we serve Jesus, so that the life of Jesus will be evident in our dying bodies. So we live in the face of death, but this has resulted in eternal life for you.

But we continue to preach because we have the same kind of faith the psalmist had when he said, "I believed in God, so I spoke." We know that God, who raised the Lord Jesus, will also raise us with Jesus and present us to himself together with you. All of this is for your benefit.

And as God's grace reaches more and more people, there will be great thanksgiving, and God will receive more and more glory.

That is why we never give up. Though our bodies are dying, our spirits are being renewed every day. For our present troubles are small and won't last very long. Yet they produce for us a glory that vastly outweighs them and will last forever! So we don't look at the troubles we can see now; rather, we fix our gaze on things that cannot be seen. For the things we see now will soon be gone, but the things we cannot see will last forever.

What A Friend We Have In Jesus

Converse

Joseph Scriven, 1819-1886　　　　　　　　　　**Charles C. Converse, 1832-1918**

What a Friend we have in Jesus, All our sins and grief's to bear!

What a priv-i-lege to carry--Ev-'rything to God in prayer!

O What peace we oft-en forfeit, O what need-less pain we bear,

All be-cause we do not car-ry-- Ev-'ry-thing to God in prayer!

Have we trials and temptations? Is there trouble anywhere?

We should nev-er be dis-cour-aged--Take it to the Lord in prayer.

Can we find a friend so faith-ful? Who will all our sor-rows share?

Je-sus knows our ev-'ry weak-ness --Take it to the Lord in prayer

Are we weak and heav-y-laden, Cum-bered with a load of care?

Pre-cious Sav-ior, still our re-fuge--Take it to the Lord in prayer.

Do thy friends de-spise, forsake thee? Take it to the Lord in prayer;

In His arms He'll take and shield thee--Thou wilt find sol-ace there.

A psalm of thanksgiving.

Psalm 100 verses 1 through five

Shout with joy to the LORD, all the earth!
Worship the LORD with gladness.
Come before him, singing with joy.
Acknowledge that the LORD is God!
He made us, and we are his.
We are his people, the sheep of his pasture.
Enter his gates with thanksgiving;
go into his courts with praise.
Give thanks to him and praise his name.
For the LORD is good.
His unfailing love continues forever,
and his faithfulness continues to each generation.

Because I am righteous In Jesus, I will see you..

When I awake, I will see you face to face and be satisfied. Psalm 17:14

Your favorite thought here: My prayers, My hopes, My dreams will be fulfilled, and I can see Jesus with continued expectations. To be with Him forever.

A prayer thought:

Lord Jesus, because of you we are never alone. Because of your mercy, allowing us time to understand and appreciate your desire to have a personal relationship with us. A relationship that your Father, full of mercy, was compelled and willing to send you to pay the debt of our sins, to conquer our sinful nature, changing it to a joyous spiritual nature, so we now can abide in you, and with you. Now we celebrate with you in your Kingdom of everlasting life, purchased by you in the sacrifice you made at the cross for us. We have been made aware of your words in scripture that speak of your willingness to die for us. In fact, according to the law of Moses, nearly everything was purified with blood.

For without the shedding of blood, there is no forgiveness. **Hebrews 9:22**

It was plainly understood by God Almighty that His only begotten Son was the only one who could purify us for eternity, since the blood of animals could not do that

Jesus answered him, I assure you, most solemnly I tell you, that unless a person is born again anew, from above, he cannot ever see (know, be acquainted with, and experience) the kingdom of God. **John 3:3**

And I will betroth thee unto me for ever; yea, I will betroth thee unto me in righteousness, and in judgment, and in loving kindness, and in mercies.

I will even betroth thee unto me in faithfulness: and thou shalt know the LORD.

Hosea 2:19-20

And they, like you, will finally recognize me as the Lord.

The Spirit of God, who raised Jesus from the dead, lives in you. And just as God raised Christ Jesus from the dead, he will give life to your mortal bodies by this same Spirit living within you. (If, indeed it lives within you.....Have you invited Him into your heart?) **Romans 8:11**

As you read this book please consider:

This book is especially printed for you. Show and tell should be at work in your life at this time.

If you have been saved, did you know that you are considered the bride of Jesus, as you received Him as your Lord and Savior? Some parts of scripture are written in the form of an analog to add meaning or substance to the article.

"Whosoever Believeth In Him!"

If Reading This Book Is Important to you? Understanding Your Part Is Important To God.

Is it your wish to develop a deep abiding relationship with God, Even onto Salvation? Then listen as you hear His abiding voice calling to you, and may these scriptures be helpful in your striving to know Him more completely.

Reaching For His Righteousness....
With A Light From His Son

If you then had a house; who would be the true builder? If you were alone in distress whose help would you need? **Psalm 127:1-2**

How can anyone protect their marriage according to Proverbs 4:4: compare this verse to..... **Psalms 119:9-11**

These verses are especially included here to make us aware of our need for a close relationship with Jesus. *To be born again* into His Kingdom! Let's face it:

If we ourselves were an army, we couldn't face the elements in our lives in this world. **God** has always been in control of this world, and He has brought us safely to this point in our lives.

Where will obeying God lead us according to **Psalm 85:10?**

Then we will win favor and a good name in the sight of God and man. **Proverbs 3:4**

Also at **Jeremiah 29:11-14.**

Do you not realize that in a race everyone runs, but only one person gets the prize? Run in such a way as to get the prize. So I run with purpose in every step. I am not just shadow boxing. I discipline my body like an athlete, training it to do what it should. Otherwise, I fear that after preaching to others I myself might be disqualified.(This was the first impact on my journey with Christ.)

1 Corinthians 9:24-27

Reaching For His Righteousness.....With The Light of The Son.

Deuteronomy 8:1-5 Do Not Forget the LORD

Be careful to follow every command I am giving you today, so that you may live and increase and may enter and possess the land that the LORD promised on oath to your forefathers. Remember how the LORD your God led you all the way in the desert these forty years, to humble you and to test you in order to know what was in your heart, whether or not you would keep his commands. *He humbled you, causing you to hunger and then feeding you with manna, which neither you nor your fathers had known,* to teach you that man does not live on bread alone but on every word that comes from the mouth of the LORD. Your clothes did not wear out and your feet did not swell during these forty years. Know then in your heart that as a man disciplines his son, so the LORD your God disciplines you. **Deuteronomy 8:1-5...**

Make a special memory note of verse 3b How can we obey if no orders are given? Isn't it wonderful that Almighty God would give us His word, and commands to follow Him?

When Love and faithfulness meet together:

Righteousness and Peace have kissed....Psalm 85:10

Chapter Two

We Should Never Be Discouraged
"Because"
His desire is for salvation (New Birth) For All

In the first Chapter we learned how God built His church and who the King is. Also, what the King came to do. How His chosen people respond to His agape love. How He became King, and why individuals have the openness, and individual desire to receive Him. He has taught us through His word how to live by doing what is right, as well as the act of forgiveness, and of knowing who your brother is with thanksgiving and love. In the following chapter we also learn why living for salvation is also a matter of individual choice. Choosing life is an individual choice, but many make this choice **without understanding the depth of it.** Even the devil believes, and trembles. When you choose life, real life in Christ that is, you are choosing an eternity with Him. This life begins the day you accept Him, inviting Him into your heart and life. You become one of His anointed children, set apart from the world. Anointed to serve him in everlasting joy. His resurrection power becomes your joy, as your heart is lifted up when His Spirit calls you. Now you are graciously placed by His mercy, love, and a total forgiveness in your new life with Christ; both now and forever.

Bobs Story as Jesus could be telling it.

Jesus said, "You have ears, Bob, but you cannot hear. And you have eyes but you cannot see. Does that news trouble you so that you refuse to consider it? To be healed, and be born again?

It took an accident with major trauma in Bob's life to restore his 'ears that hear and eyes that see.' (It doesn't need to be that way)

You see, according to God's plan when we came into this life we were only visitors traveling through." Sin blinds. But being baptized and confirmed gave me the confidence of canceled sin. I thought that the sights and human desires were part of Gods' plan for my life. Just be a good person and the eyes of God would cast approval from Him for my life. Deceived and double-deceived! I left Christ hanging in the walls of our home. Even in my bedroom where I could see the good shepherd every day and night. Always knocking on my door with love and a calling to "Come."

"Bob spent many years here on earth enjoying all the sights, committing himself to hell when heaven was really his home.

All of us possess gifts from God so precious that our sense of reason is unable to describe it until the Blessed Father reveals it, but not without searching. **Jeremiah 29:13–14** announces this truth: If you look for me in earnest, you will find me when you seek me with all your heart. I will be found by you,' says the Lord."

"I will end your captivity to the devil and give you the abundant life I promised to all who believe. I will gather you out of the world you chose to live in, and bring you home again to the people I purposed you for. There is an urgency to tell the world about life and death, considering that life is so short and the fact that eternity is forever."

Just as God promised, I Bob continue to declare in my own words these thoughts:

Most people are totally unaware of the beautiful things that God has prepared for all those who love Him. Would He have sent His Only Son to die in such misery and suffering if that death wasn't designed by His incredible mercy to change the direction of our lives and to establish a permanent relationship with Him? He gave us a life in birth; then a new birth in life. "It is finished." Jesus' words while on the cross. Amazing words to all who take the time to hear them repeated in their lives and hearts forever. Your sins were forgiven two thousand years ago, and they belong to everyone who believes and receives Jesus as their God and Savior. And, in so doing, your spiritual eyes and ears have been healed and restored to a vision and a hope in these words from the cross.

My urgency for sharing the "Greatest Story Ever Told" was delivered to me with a great passion from Jesus Himself, because it isn't His desire that anyone should perish. He loves us through all suffering and death, and He Himself took it upon Himself to suffer the most. Since He is God, death could not hold or destroy Him. He passes that power on to all of us who have our eyes and ears restored and are looking for Him, now able to praise and worship Him forever.

Timothy's Responsibility

Timothy, my son, You too, Bob, and all who feel responsible; here are my instructions for you, based on the prophetic words spoken about you earlier. May they help you fight well in the Lord's battles. Cling to your faith in Christ, and keep your conscience clear. *For some people have deliberately violated their consciences; as a result, their faith has been shipwrecked.*

1Timothy 18-19 The next day after the visit of the Pharisees from Jerusalem , John looked up and saw Jesus coming toward him. In the thrill and excitement of that moment, he cried out,

"Behold! The Lamb of God who bears the sin of the world." The lamb was a sacrificial animal among the Jews. God had taught His chosen people to slay a lamb and to sprinkle its blood as a sacrifice. The lamb was killed as a substitute and its blood shed so that sins might be forgiven. However the blood of the lambs slain during the OT period did not put away sin. Those lambs were pictures or types, pointing forward to the fact that God would one day provide a Lamb who would actually take away the sin. All down through the years, Godly Jews had waited for the coming of this Lamb of God.

When he said that Jesus bears the sin of the world, he did not mean that everyone's sins are therefore forgiven. The death of Christ was great enough in value to pay for the sins of the whole world, but only those sinners who received the Lord Jesus as Savior and journey with Him are forgiven through His word. **John 1:30-31**

I was 41 when the Lord called me into His presence to be "Born Again." *Confirmation didn't save me, for it can't until one is born again.*

Is it so hard to totally give your heart to Jesus, when He died so that you would? Let's Face it! It is, but eternal life with Christ awaits those who do.

If you could see Jesus over the hill of your life, would you totally commit to Him then?

"Come"

Don't let your hearts be troubled. Trust in God, and trust also in me. There is more than enough room in my Father's home. If this were not so, would I have told you that I am going to prepare a place for you? When everything is ready, I will come and get you, so that you will always be with me where I am. **John 14:1-3** This book has its beginning and ending in the truth of God's Word. Brought to life by the power of His Spirit through the gift of faith **(the "uncovering of the veil," (see 2 Corinthians 3:16).** We talked about the veil earlier on page 42. Scripture: Yes, down to this [very] day whenever Moses is read about in the bible, a veil lies upon the human mind and hearts. But whenever a person turns [in repentance] to the Lord, the veil is stripped off and taken away. These verses lay in a thankful position in my heart, ever reminding me of the grace and mercy of Jesus.

He took me in! Bless Him! You are worthy of my praises.

My Lord and My God! **2 Corinthians 3:15-16**

Faith will find its stimulus in salvation at the cross where He died and rose again to bring life to all who understand and believe the joy and purpose of His life, while giving it up for their sake.

His Word, along with songs and poems, are laid out in this book in order to draw you close while surrendering to Jesus Christ, the central figure of these writings. The truth of God's Word is indeed a testimony of His love for man. Needless to say, I am happy and joyful to be able to share this new life, and the manifestation of His love, which he sent to myself and ultimately our family. He is faithful in all His promises; He did indeed remove the veil which was covering my eyes with unbelief, and kept me from enjoying a close relationship with Him. I treasure the words He has spoken to His children because they come to us from His heart through the Holy Bible, delivered so beautifully to us by His Spirit.

And it shall be that whoever shall call upon the name of the Lord [invoking, adoring, and worshiping the Lord--Christ] shall be saved.

Acts 2:21

Because God Himself is the author of the Bible, He revealed it to us by His own Spirit, because He is the Spirit of Truth. It is my prayer that your heart will be opened by His loving power to the promises that God has designed and directed especially toward you, and that you will incline your ears and heart to His wisdom and understanding for the salvation of your soul.

Like me, you may also have always had a conscious awareness of God and can testify that you have had a soft heart for Jesus…call it love if you will. Even so, I know for me, the first 41 years of my life I was lost and headed straight for hell, while believing with all my heart I was going to heaven. However, Jesus was not living in my heart, because I controlled it, instead of letting His beautiful words fan it into flame.

But how could I have been so mistaken? I was baptized and went through confirmation. Inwardly I thought I was a good person. I went to church and was a church member. I thought I trusted in Jesus, but I realize now that it was on my terms, and that He wasn't involved with His will or commands for my life. He needed to melt my heart. Putting it in human terms, "I lived for Bob" and apart from a feeble faith, I did the things that pleased me. **In Proverbs 14:12** He told me plainly; "There is a way that seems right to a man, Bob, but it ends in death."

Reaching For His Righteousness…..With The Light Of the Son

2 Chronicles7:14 A lowly person's spirit praying to the exalted King and depending on Him completely

God knows the plans He has for us and He wants us to know them as well, Do not look to people or things. Your creator has His own plans for you, and I.

Jeremiah 29:8-14

1 Corinthians:12:12-31 There are many different people serving the Lord by His commands. Recognize them and love them as yourself for their work is in the Lord.

Hebrews 1:6 Jesus is ruler of all things. God's purpose is for us to be obedient to Him. Even the angels are subject to His Godliness.

1 Peter 2:2 Do you want to be saved? Be like little babies who depend on God's word like babies depend on the milk and care of their mother's.

2 Corinthians 13:5 Search your heart! Is Jesus living there and in full control.

The next pages have verses in scripture that command my attention, and yours.

Reaching for His Righteousness...With The Light His Son offers freely.

Deuteronomy 4:4-8.... Is it possible to obey God in all His ways without a good knowledge of who He is? How can we really know God? Check out **John 14:6** and

John 3:3 They give us a complete clue. Jesus is like the Father, in person and in authority. We must grow to become more and more like Him. Obedience is the key.

Revelations 3:20 Also Psalm 119:9-11 Let your life be like His life. Perfectly abundant and free.

Peter1:22 Obey God's word, so you can love your brother's and sister's properly.

John 14:21 Both the Father and the Son will love you if you obey God's word.

Galatians 5:7-8 You were running a good race until the one who cut in on you.

Galatians 5:16-17 The Spirit and the sinful nature are at war with one another, so obey the Spirit's calling.

John 14:24 Anyone who does not love me will not obey my teaching. The words you hear me say are not my own. They belong to the Father who sent me.

"Come".....continued

Protect yourself by coming!

The child of God is guarded by the power of God for salvation ready to be revealed in the last time. **1ˢᵗ Peter 1:5** Consider this verse even more positive than you would a ticket to your favorite event. Are you one of the many? Are you eagerly waiting? Is He saying "Come" so that you too will be saved.

Your body will be changed and glorified, and be forever free from sin, sickness, and death. This future tense of salvation also includes the time when saints will return to the earth with Christ and will be clearly shown to be children of God. **1John 3.2**

The Holy Spirit continually invites people to believe and come to Him. What are your thoughts as you meditate on the study above and the invitation to 'come'.

Please pray these words of supplication with me: Heavenly Father.....In your book of **John, Chapter 15:5** you tell us plainly that without you, we can do nothing. The word 'nothing' seems so empty to us. We confess that we are apt to do everything without you. Help us to remove the ego in our lives. Show us our need to obey the way your only begotten Son, the Lamb Of God, obeyed in the fullness of his love and joy for you. Make our love so complete for you that we will spend much time in your Word, and that its natural course will lead us into a more complete obedience and will be contagious to the many lives around us. In the name of the our Lord and Savior Jesus, who with the Father and the faithful Holy Spirit, live in us forever..... AMEN

The Throne Of God Or A Wishing Well

When I was living without the Lord, and looking here and there,

I often made a wish—or two—and seemed to really care…

I wished for many things—that others did possess,

Hadn't heard about God's mercy, or even the wilderness…

I didn't know my thoughts were sin, an insult to our Lord

Just wanted to possess—those things which I adored

I didn't know He died for me, felt I was pretty good,

Pleasure was my purpose—producing things it should...

Until the day of Son-shine—replaced the dazzling stars,

And in the brightness of the Son, how He wiped away my scars

It was a day of joy—when He came to call on me,

And I rose in all His righteousness, to see what I could see

He led me through His Word—imparting it to me,

And in my very presence, drew me close to Him and Thee…

My heart fell to its knees, by the wonder of His plan,

That He would die in misery, to hold me in His hand…

Poem by Bob Bowman

If you do come, "Listen" to the edification and warning that He spells out.

"Listen, O heavens, and I will speak! Hear, O earth, the words that I say!

Let my teaching fall on you like rain; let my speech settle like dew.

Let my words fall like rain on tender grass, like gentle showers on

Young plants. I will proclaim the name of the Lord; how glorious our God!

He is the Rock; his deeds are perfect. Everything he does is just and fair.

He is a faithful God who does no wrong; how just and upright he is!

"But they have acted corruptly toward him; when they act so perversely,

are they really his children? They are a deceitful and twisted generation.

Is this the way you repay the Lord, you foolish and senseless people?

Isn't he your Father who created you? Has he not made you and

established you?

Remember the days of long ago; think about the generations past. Ask

your father, and he will inform you. Inquire of your elders,

and they will tell you.

When the Most High assigned lands to the nations, when he divided up

the human race, he established the boundaries of the peoples, according

to the number in his heavenly court." **Deuteronomy 32**

Regarding the above and its position here at this time, I offer the following.

The Apostle Paul reminds us that the book (Deuteronomy) has a message for us as well as for Israel. In commenting on **Deuteronomy 25:4** he says that it was written altogether for our sakes. **1 Corinthians 9:10.** The book is rich in exhortation, which can be summed up in the verbs of **Deuteronomy 5:1:** "Hear.....Learn.....Keep and do."

Moses is credited for the writings of Deuteronomy except for the time of his departure to be with the Lord.

I do not hide your righteousness in my heart; I speak of your faithfulness and your saving help. I do not conceal your love and faithfulness from the great assembly.

Psalm 40:10

For This exact reason He tells us repeatedly: I am the way, The Truth and the Life and no one can come to the Father except by me. **John 14:6**

The Real Everlasting Joy.
This Poem relates the joy of the person who has found Him.

What a glorious feeling a player has when the final gun does sound,

And victory is in his hand as his teammates gather around.

They lift his feet up off the ground and carry him away,

His heart swells up inside him, a hero for a day…

'Twas attention he deserved, his heart was in the game.

With a dedicated effort, he earned that day of fame.

That is how I feel about Jesus and the battle that He has won,

Alone He came to save the world, what a joy for those who "Come."

While His Father placed His faith in Him, our Jesus had the will,

To save a world of sinners, shedding His blood on Calvary's Hill.

And when they raised Him on the cross, a hero in His Father's eye,

So lovingly He murmured, "Father, forgive them when I die…

For they know not what they're doing." His words now oh so clear,

And I think about my hero, as I listen to them cheer…

'Tis no wonder that I'm satisfied, being called to play His game,

To appreciate these heroes….. and recognize their fame.

I'll tell you oh so dearly, 'bout Christ, who holds my hand each day,

Never doubting about His presence, imparting thrills along my way…

Yeah, now I have the Victory, where the game of life is found.

Not in my hand, but in my heart, Lord Jesus I have crowned.

May these words draw others near, and His salvation will abound.

Poem By Bob Bowman

Born anew into an inheritance which is beyond the reach of change and decay imperishable, unsullied and unfading, reserved in heaven for you, Who are being guarded garrisoned by God's power through your faith till you fully inherit that final salvation that is ready to be revealed for you in the last time. **1Peter 1:4-5**

If you do "Come" be sure of your Confidence, Trust, and Hope! Let your life hinge on Jesus residing in you. For then you can't be trusting yourself as you see Him waiting.

They sent some of their disciples, along with the supporters of Herod, to meet with him. "Teacher, they said, we know how honest you are. You teach the way of God truthfully. You are impartial and don't play favorites. Now tell us what you think about this: Is it right to pay taxes to Caesar or not?" The Christians proof for not being unequally yoked.

But Jesus knew their evil motives.

"You hypocrites! He said. "Why are you trying to trap me? Here, show me the coin used for the tax." When they handed him a Roman coin, he asked,

"Whose picture and title are stamped on it?" "Caesar's," they replied. "Well, then," he said, "give to Caesar what belongs to Caesar, and give to God what belongs to God." His reply amazed them, and they went away. **Matthew 22:16-22**

Looking back: We have physical attributes to hear God speak to us; or in His mercy we can be shown or told…No one will have an excuse. Praise be to God for our evangelists A. We have spiritual responsibilities. B. His commands. The Holy Spirit has given us the truth. C. a definite beckoning to be involved. ('come') What is there in this life that has a joyful compatibility with 'A Life In Christ'. A wish or a promise. A joy or a heartache.

Things that I found to be true of Christians:

They receive Jesus Christ into their heart and life.

Also Join a bible preaching and teaching church.

They begin to study the bible everyday.

And they develop fellowship with other Christians.

Developing their knowledge of Him, who He is and that He alone is worthy of all praise, adoration and counseling with prayer.

Do not be unequally yoked with unbelievers….You will know them by their fruits…You will understand why it brings tears to your cheeks..

The bible states clearly why *as Jesus encountered passion and pain that He wept.*

Let your heart die to the world with it's style of living, and you will see a world of dying people to help. To die is to live; And to live is to die.

It is written: "I believed; therefore I have spoken. With that same spirit of faith we also believe and therefore speak, because we know that the one who raised the Lord Jesus from the dead will also raise us with Jesus and present us with you in his presence. All this is for your benefit, so that the grace that is reaching more and more people may cause thanksgiving to overflow to the glory of God.

2 Corinthians 4:13-15

Chapter Three

Choose Life..... And..... Walk With Jesus

The actual process for the word's "To Come."

Understanding who He is, and what He does for those who "Choose Life" is one of the mysteries of the Holy Spirit. For every struggle in life, He is with us, never leaving or forsaking us. He is always near. Jesus knows our longings and is always there as we trust in Him for His wisdom and power to control our lives. Open your heart for Him inviting Him in today, as the Holy Spirit leads you, even now.

Have You Heard The Story OF Jesus ?

The Bible is God's Home. Every book in the Bible is the street where He lives on. And every verse in the Bible is the room where He is staying. He is ever present. The room He dwells in is for our particular need. Thus, we are never without Him according to our own faith and needs. He always rejoices when we call on Him. Then He transfers that joy to our hearts.

What a Savior, and who can live without Him? Not a single person in the entire world that He created for His own purpose.

Scripture testifies in many places that we can claim to belong to God, even when we are not following Him.

The above is one of the reasons for writing this book. Of course, First foremost is to bring honor to God. **Faith Amplified for others to see and follow!**

While His gospel is preached.

In the surroundings of the world, we see many people going to and fro. Everyone seems to have a mission of their own. Is it possible as we endeavor to be their friends, even as a stranger, to tell them about a Savior who wants to be their dearest and most loving friend? I detect a melody that has impacted my life so much that I want everyone's eyes to be upon Jesus, to receive Him, to learn about His love for them, so that they too may spend eternity with Him. He wants to come and get everyone who seeks Him, who find their need for Him, so that He would be with them forever when their time is ready. I don't believe that means when the world comes to an end. I believe He is calling you today to believe in Him, and to give your life to Him in dedication and service, so that when everything about you is ready, His love and mercy will carry you home to Him. It may be one of His angels that escorts you to Him, but nevertheless, He wants you to be 'Where He Is.' Now, can you imagine a personal love and relationship with God Almighty forever? You are chosen and called to Jesus who became your dear brother while shedding His blood on Calvary for you. Are you covered by His blood? How does anyone become covered by His blood? For me it happened in **Revelations 3:19-20** His words to me were:"If anyone hears my voice and opens the door, I will come in and eat with him, and he with me." Quite different to the invitations I knew without Him, which were almost always full of the liquid diet instead of words of comfort and joy. I soon learned that my dearest friendships came from God's Word and not from the world. As I was separated from the world environment, there were lost friendships that I missed. Yet I was called, so I called people to join me in fellowship with the real leader of the universe in a faith that would carry all of us to His loving arms forever. This brings us to a point.

Have you experienced the abundant life while losing your own life that you have given up for Jesus?

Below is an overview that God's word lays out to help support us as we attempt to serve our living Savior in the continual mode of our personal relationship with Him. We just need to give Him the reins that direct our lives.

Jesus is the same yesterday, today, and forever. So do not be attracted by strange, new ideas. Your spiritual strength comes from God's special favor, not from ceremonial rules about food, which don't help those who follow them.

Hebrews 13:8

We have an altar from which the priests in the Tabernacle have no right to eat.. but Jesus suffered and died outside the city gates to make his people holy by means of his own blood. So let us go out to him, outside the camp, and bear the disgrace he bore. For this world is not our permanent home; we are looking forward to a home yet to come.

Choosing..... Life..... Or..... Death

Therefore, let us offer through Jesus a continual sacrifice of praise to God, proclaiming our allegiance to his name. And don't forget to do good and to share with those in need. These are the sacrifices that please God.

Obey your spiritual leaders, and do what they say. Their work is to watch over your souls, and they are accountable to God. Give them reason to do this with joy and not with sorrow. That would certainly not be for your benefit.

Pray for us, for our conscience is clear and we want to live honorably in everything we do. And especially pray that I will be able to come back to you soon.

Now may the God of peace—who brought us up from the dead by our Lord Jesus, the great Shepherd of the sheep, and ratified an eternal covenant with his blood, may he equip you with all you need for doing his will. May he produce in you, through the power of Jesus, every good thing that is pleasing to Him. All glory to Him forever and ever! Amen. **Hebrews 13:10-21**

How does one give up his own life for Christ? Or should we say, To give up this temporary existence to add an eternity with Christ with all His blessings? It's a wonderful life has no comparison to this life in Christ that comes freely through Him. Anything given up returns just as Jesus said it would in the flow of abundance from God, as you turn toward God and your neighbor.

Then Jesus said to his disciples, "If any of you wants to be my follower, you must turn from your selfish ways, take up your cross, and follow me. If you try to hang on to your life, you will lose it. But if you give up your life for my sake, you will save it. And what do you benefit if you gain the whole world but lose your own soul? Is anything worth more than your soul? **Mathew 16:24-26**

See what **Revelations 3:19-20** has to say about this question. Doesn't that sound personal? Compare that with **Isaiah 59:2** It is important that everyone does that.

Sounds like He wants our hearts to live in His heart **John 15:5**..... Jesus is the only answer. I found that out when I invited Jesus into my sinful heart. P.S. He died to change it!

The Believers Form a Community:

All the believers devoted themselves to the apostles' teaching, and to fellowship, and to sharing in meals (including the Lord's Supper and to prayer. A deep sense of awe came over them all, and the apostles performed many miraculous signs and wonders. And all the believers met together in one place and shared everything they had. They sold their property and possessions and shared the money with those in need. They worshiped together at the Temple each day, met in homes for the Lord's Supper, and shared their meals with great joy and generosity all the while praising God and enjoying the goodwill of all the people. And each day the Lord added to their fellowship those who were being saved. **Acts 2:42-47**

"This command I am giving you today is not too difficult for you to understand, and it is not beyond your reach. It is not kept in heaven, so distant that you must ask, 'Who will go up to heaven and bring it down so we can hear it and obey?' It is not kept beyond the sea, so far away that you must ask, 'Who will cross the sea to bring it to us so we can hear it and obey?' No, the message is very close at hand; it is on your lips and in your heart so that you can obey it."

"Now listen! Today I am giving you a choice between life and death, between prosperity and disaster. For I command you this day to love the Lord your God and to keep His commands, decrees, and regulations by walking in His ways. If you do this, you will live and multiply, and the Lord your God will bless you and the land you are about to enter and occupy."

Strong and powerful is the opinion of the author Bob: Plant your feet on the rock, which is Jesus, and lean forward.

Be careful that you do not refuse to listen to the one who is speaking. For if the people of Israel did not escape when they refused to listen to Moses, the earthly messenger, we will certainly not escape if we reject the one who speaks to us from heaven! When God spoke from Mount Sinai his voice shook the earth, but now he makes another promise: "Once again I will shake not only the earth but the heavens also." This means that all of creation will be shaken and removed, so that only unshakable things will remain. **Hebrews 12:25-27**

"Today I have given you the choice between life and death, between blessings and curses. Now I call on heaven and earth to witness the choice you make. Oh, that you would choose life, so that you and your descendants might live! You can make this choice by loving the Lord your God, obeying him, and committing yourself firmly to Him. This is the key to your life. And if you love and obey the Lord, you will live long in the land the Lord swore to give your ancestors Abraham, Isaac, and Jacob."

Deuteronomy 30:11-20

God's Plan: Living Your Life With Jesus Living In You. Your second birth.

John.3:3

God is able to make you strong, just as the Good News says. It is the message about Jesus Christ and his Plan for you Gentiles, a plan kept secret from the beginning of time. But now as the prophets foretold and as the Eternal God has commanded, that this message is made known to all Gentiles everywhere, so that they might believe and obey Christ. To God, who alone is wise, be glory forever through Jesus Christ.

Romans 16:25-27

And since we are His children, we are His heirs. In fact, together with Christ we are heirs of God's glory. But if we are to share His glory, we also must share in His suffering. **Romans 8:17**

Jesus, The Son Of God.

Many religions acknowledge Jesus as a great prophet, healer and teacher. But Jesus never claimed to be a great prophet, healer or teacher.

He was God's Son.....incarnate! Incarnate means Christ is God in the flesh. Yes, God came to us in the flesh, that we might know Him, so that by believing we may be changed to be like He is and become a living spirit in the flesh.

John 5:39-45 You diligently study] the Scriptures because you think that by them you possess eternal life. These are the Scriptures that testify about me, **40** yet you refuse to come to me to have life. A partial view…Read through 45. Also check out the verses below:

John 14:6-7…If you know Jesus you will know the Father as well.

Isaiah 53:10….. (please check it out) God was pleased to watch His Son suffer, so He could save you and I….What deeper cost could He incur?

"Jesus replied, "I tell you the truth, unless you are born again, you cannot see the Kingdom of God." "What do you mean?" exclaimed Nicodemus. "How can an old man go back into his mother's womb and be born again?" Jesus replied, "I assure you, no one can enter the Kingdom of God without being born of water and the Spirit.

John 3:3

The Narrow Gate: "You can enter God's Kingdom only through the narrow gate. The highway to hell is broad, and its gate is wide for the many who choose that way. But the gateway to life is very narrow and the road is difficult, and only a few ever find it.

Matthew 7:13-14

New Bodies,

For we know that when this earthly tent we live in is taken down (that is, when we die and leave this earthly body), we will have a house in heaven, an eternal body made for us by God Himself and not by human hands. We grow weary in our present bodies, and we long to put on our heavenly bodies like new clothing. For we will put on heavenly bodies; we will not be spirits without bodies. While we live in these earthly bodies, we groan and sigh, but it's not that we want to die and get rid of these bodies that clothe us. Rather, we want to put on our new bodies so that these dying bodies will be swallowed up by life.

God Himself has prepared us for this, and as a guarantee He has given us His Holy Spirit.

So we are always confident, even though we know that as long as we live in these bodies we are not at home with the Lord. For we live by believing and not by seeing. Yes, we are fully confident, and we would rather be away from these earthly bodies, for then we will be at home with the Lord. So whether we are here in this body or away from this body, our goal is to please Him. For we must all stand before Christ to be judged. We will each receive whatever we deserve for the good or evil we have done in this earthly body. **2 Corinthians 5:6-10**

We Are God's Ambassadors:

Because we understand our fearful responsibility to the Lord, we work hard to persuade others. God knows we are sincere, and I hope you know this, too. Are we commending ourselves to you again? No, we are giving you a reason to be proud of us so you can answer those who brag about having a spectacular ministry rather than having a sincere heart. If it seems we are crazy, it is to bring glory to God. And if we are in our right minds, it is for your benefit. Either way, Christ's love controls us. Since we believe that Christ died for all, we also believe that we have all died to our old life. He died for everyone. **2 Corinthians 5:11-15**

The Kingdom Of God

One of the benefits of submitting to God, as you invite Jesus into your heart, is that you become citizens of His Kingdom at that very moment of your life. Heirs apparent to His riches in glory and are instantly known by God as Heaven Bound. Now submitting to His will, and His ways, while you search for ways to serve and grow to be more like Jesus.... remembering now and forever that you have become the full spiritual brother of Jesus..... Partners In Christ ! What you are now gifted to see is what Jesus has spoken on your benefit in His word. You now have a wonderful new job, a new boss and above all, you are a favorite son to be watched, as you do His will.

Nothing in this life or world can possible compare to that. He has been my boss, my friend, my savior, my counselor, my God Almighty and my joy for 35 years at this writing. Yes, He is my greatest possession, and the anchor that holds me close to Him. He is always near me and never condemns me while rebuking and disciplining me as I remain in fellowship with Him. I would be very lonesome without His companionship.

So that those who receive His new life will no longer live for themselves. Instead, they will live for Christ, who died and was raised for them.

Reaching for His Righteousness.....In The Light Of he Son

Search the scripture's and look for your observation, Your application, and your prayer's for what you read. See if these verses are saying, "Lord, your will and your way."

Record them in your heart for safe keeping…

Matthew 18:9-10 Jesus said, "I have not lost anyone God has given me." Read also John **6:39:**

1 John 2:15-17

Matthew7:13-14

Deuteronomy 8:3 God teaches us that man doesn't live on bread alone, but by every word that comes from the mouth of God

James 2:9-11, also 19 & 20 It is also very helpful to examine all of the above verses. Write down your own thoughts confirming & aligning them with God's word.

I will give you all the proof you want that Christ speaks through me. Christ is not weak when he deals with you; he is powerful among you. Although he was crucified in weakness, he now lives by the power of God. We, too, are weak, just as Christ was, but when we deal with you we will be alive with him and will have God's power.

Examine yourselves to see if your faith is genuine. Test yourselves. Surely you know that Jesus Christ is among you; if not, you have failed the test of genuine faith. As you test yourselves, I hope you will recognize that we have not failed the test of apostolic authority.

We pray to God that you will not do what is wrong by refusing our correction. I hope we won't need to demonstrate our authority when we arrive. Do the right thing before we come—even if that makes it look like we have failed to demonstrate our authority. For we cannot oppose the truth, but must always stand for the truth. We are glad to seem weak if it helps show that you are actually strong. We pray that you will become mature. **2 Corinthians 13:3-9**

Remember, we are choosing this life to die within us , in order for His life to live within us!

Our Lord tells us that we can't Serve Him without giving up the world,

And its' value system; Lest we begin to have more than one God.

"But anyone who hears my teaching and doesn't obey it is foolish, like a person who builds a house on sand. When the rains and floods come and the winds beat against that house, it will collapse with a mighty crash." When Jesus had finished saying these things, the crowd were amazed at his teaching, for He taught with real authority—quite unlike their teachers of religious law." **Matthew 7:26-29**

Real Love is obedience in action:

Truth, Discipline, and Sharing His Word

You have a child who walks out into the street after repeated warnings. You wonder, "Is it rebellion, forgetfulness, or a challenge to the limits you have set?" In our relationships with God, we sometimes let our contrary reasoning lead us into sin; which angers God. He calls it disgusting, or, using His terms in the book of Leviticus, it is an abomination. Knowing God's Word is the remedy—obeying is the only solution.

In Matthew 23 Jesus mentions seven ways to guarantee God's anger, which are often called the "seven woes of God."

1. Matthew 23:13–14: Not entering the Kingdom of Heaven and not allowing others to enter the Kingdom of Heaven.

2. Matthew 23:15: Converting people to be like ourselves and thus leading them away from God. [15]"Woe to you, teachers of the law and Pharisees, you hypocrites! You travel over land and sea to win a single convert, and when he becomes one, you make him twice as much a son of hell as you are.

3. Matthew 23:16–22: Blindly leading God's people to follow man-made traditions instead of God's Word. What does this say about false teachers? Aren't they liars?

4. Matthew 23:23–24: Involving yourself in every last detail and ignoring what is really important—following Jesus in justice, mercy, and faithfulness.

5. Matthew 23:25–26: "Keeping up appearances" while your private world is corrupt.

6. Matthew 23:27–28: Acting "spiritual" to cover up sin. Are these liars?

7. Matthew 23:29: Pretending to have learned from past history, but your present behavior proves you have learned nothing. These seven statements about the religious leaders of Jesus' day must have been spoken with a mixed tone of judgment and sorrow. They are strong and unforgettable. And they are still a practice of religion that we forget that God is also concerned with mercy, real love, and forgiveness.

Reaching for righteousness....In the light of the Son.

Prayerfully consider the "Seven Woes" and list your comments here below.

1.

2.

3.

4.

5.

6.

7.

As everyone can tell, I have mentioned a personal relationship with Jesus quite often in order to highlight the name of this book "A Chosen Life Study."

The name itself alludes to something special. In all honesty, as we look at the seven woes, we all find ourselves guilty. If that is true (and it is) how can I be satisfied with my life and at the same time be at peace with God. Please let me explain…at least for myself.

Then Jesus said, "Come to me", all of you who are weary and carry heavy burdens, and I will give you rest. Here again is the invitation to come.

Take my yoke upon you. Let me teach you, because I am humble and gentle at heart, and you will find rest for your souls.

For my yoke is easy to bear, and the burden I give you is light." **Matthew 11:28-29**

A. Is it a burden he gives us? **B.** And where does the peace that passes all understanding come from? **C.** What do we need to do to find it?

I believe all these questions are swallowed up in victory when we take the first step.

"Come!"

The Holy Spirit is God's will for all. That they may enjoy His word.

Are you worthy? Will you walk daily with Jesus? Worthy means to accept His call & His Grace that flows with it….Then you begin to listen to His voice… while finding yourself immersed in the Bible.

You will find that a believer almost instantly becomes involved with Christ. Then with it comes a warmth that keeps leading us to the heart of God. Any ill feelings or hardness that you had for our fellowman is brought before our Lord, and His gracious will **changes** the entire relationship, and we begin to hear the words of that great song. 'It only takes a spark to get a fire going.' Of course the key to all of this is the Lord's gracious Spirit that keeps leading us triumphantly through His word for the glory of His name, and the salvation of our soul.

It is my belief that many people are unaware of the process of being heaven-bound.

God is merciful with an abundant love, as well as an absolute love for all men. While He has no favorites, He is still a jealous God. His jealousy doesn't mean He will stop loving anyone that hasn't committed their life to Him. His love is described as an agape love which simply means He doesn't require your love in order for Him to love you. But He keeps seeking an opportunity to draw you to Him, so you find yourself helpless not to love Him as your first love. The more you learn about Him, and yourself, the more you love and commit yourself to Him. *(Well done Holy Spirit....Spirit of God....In our humility we ask that you keep speaking to us.)*

Points to ponder...(Is your faith full and ready to accept and react to John 1:10-18..... Example: Check out the word birth in these verses and see when and where it comes from.

10. He was in the world, and though the world was made through him, the world did not recognize him.

11. He came to that which was his own, but his own did not receive him.

12. Yet to all who received him, to those who believed in his name, he gave the right to become children of God.

13. Children born not of natural descent nor of human decision or a husband's will,. but born of God

14. The Word became flesh and made his dwelling among us. We have seen his glory, the glory of the One and Only, who came from the Father, full of grace and truth.

15. John testifies concerning him. He cries out, saying, "This was he of whom I said, 'He who comes after me has surpassed me because he was before me.'

16. From the fullness of his grace we have all received one blessing after another.

17. For the law was given through Moses; grace and truth came through Jesus Christ.

18. No one has ever seen God, but God the One and Only, who is at the Father's. side, has made him known

John 8:12 The Validity of Jesus' Testimony: When Jesus spoke again to the people, he said, **"I am the light of the world.** Whoever follows me will never walk in darkness, but will have the light of life." **John 11:25-26** Jesus said to her, "I am the resurrection and the life. He who believes in me will live, even though he dies; **26** and whoever lives and believes in me will never die. "Do you believe this?"

John 14:6-7 Jesus answered, "I am the way and the truth and the life. No one comes to the Father except through me. **7** If you really knew me, you would know my Father as well. From now on, you do know him and have seen him."

Revelation 2:10 Do not be afraid of what you are about to suffer. I tell you, the devil will put some of you in prison to test you, and you will suffer persecution for ten days. Be faithful, even to the point of death, and I will give you the crown of life.

A psalm of David:

Keep me safe, O God, for I have come to you for refuge I said to the Lord, "You are my Master!
Every good thing I have comes from you."
The godly people in the land
are my true heroes! I take pleasure in them!
Troubles multiply for those who chase after other gods.
I will not take part in their sacrifices of blood
or even speak the names of their gods. Lord, you alone are my inheritance, my cup of blessing. You guard all that is mine The land you have given me is a pleasant land What a wonderful inheritance! **Psalm 16:1-6**

Chapter Four

A Chosen Life

Looking ahead: We have all heard the story of Jesus? How God's word works and how it explains the truth? Did you *comprehend* the part in John chapter one, under the heading "Come" in the verses of John 1:10-18....He tells us about "The word '*Born*' as we find it in verse 13?" And then how it is connected to life and light in verse four of chapter one. Then also in John 8:12 under the validity of Jesus Testimony where a complete analogy of His testimony includes Him as "The light of the world." As a side note to that, there will be no sun for the one's who live in heaven. Jesus will be our light for eternity. That is just one of the reason's why we need Jesus, because…..

There Is Hope In The Messiah

Paul affirms the humanity and divinity of Christ. By so doing he reveals the heart of the Good News, "The great mystery of Our Faith" (the secret of how we become Godly) "Appeared in the flesh" (Jesus was a man); "Was shown to be righteous by the Spirit" (Jesus is the basis of our being right with God)….Jesus resurrection showed that the Holy Spirit's Power was in him. (Romans 8:11) . "Was seen by the Angels:" and was taken up Into Heaven."…..Jesus is divine. We cannot please God on our own; We must depend on Christ. **Commentary on 1 Timothy 3:14-16**

Hope in Our Awesome God

And The Heart Of A Promise Keeper

When we depart from this life, you can write these words in stone,

that we saw Jesus here on earth; we were never left alone.

He came to us through longings, in garments oh so white

and changed our darkness into day, His glory was so bright,

He asked us to come near Him while He gave us this command

placing a peace within our hearts He took us by the hand.

Go and speak with boldness so all the world will know

that sin does have a penalty, in death its fetters glow.

He brought us comfort, strength, and joy; in fears He gave us peace.

we knew that when He called us, this life we had would cease.

So we began to follow Him, for we knew that we had died.

then peace within was multiplied when we were crucified.

He longs for you to know Him, and He is your true friend;

to stand beside you every hour, His peace will never end.

But you must turn and recognize He's calling you today,

responding with your heart and soul, His Word you must obey.

He doesn't want just service, with movements to and fro,

without a loving, contrite heart, so all the world will know

That when He bowed His head in death, in agonizing pain,

the world could be forgiven, by believing in His name.

And if His calling you believe, by opening your heart

to receive Him, God and Savior, from this world be set apart.

Then you will know His power and His presence from above,

and you can share His precious gift with your family dearly loved…

Poem By Bob Bowman

Jesus Is our Light and Life.

Come along with me. Let's find this man from Galilee. He is Almighty God. Walk with Him and listen to Him until you've taken up your stand. Then soon you'll want to talk to Him as He takes you by the hand.

The solution to our willful disobedience is the life and light of Jesus Christ coming into our lives, and our becoming children of God.

I began my new life in Christ with His Spirit in May of 1972. Jesus gave me a longing for Him and I answered His call when He ask me to stop being disobedient and let Him come into my life, in **Revelations 3:19-20.** I was convinced that I belonged to Him, and that He belonged to me. My reasoning: How did I get Here? And for what reason?

Respond to these important bible verses:

Revelation 3:19-20 (challenge and response) Open eye, Come as you hear Him call.

Psalm 40:1-3 Seeing God at work is believing in His mercy.

John14:6 Jesus is the only way.

Four short months later, in September 1972,

I began to experience a growth in the Holy Spirit and the tenderness of His calling. Although I had doubts He used them to increase my faith.

At that time I was asked to be the Superintendent of the Sunday School, and I joyfully accepted. I also became involved teaching a sixth grade Sunday class with one of my sons as a student. That was one of the joys of my life…Wow! I could just see and feel the hand of Jesus walking and working with me. Excitement galore.

One of the verses that began my longing for Him, with His love surrounding me, was

1 Peter 2:2….Like newborn babies, crave pure spiritual milk, so that by it you may grow up in your salvation, now that you have tasted that the Lord is good.

My reflection with human and spiritual comparisons: Decision times come quickly. They come and go. Are you sound and stable, connected to Christ?

Analogy: You're up to the plate. The bases are loaded! You are a natural 400 hitter, but the pressure is on…what are your thoughts? Transform that into your thinking regarding **1 Peter 2:2** in a spiritual way. (Without the confidence that God will give you, you cannot crave His Word.

But God wants you to have it, the same way you wanted and needed milk when you were a baby.) Look for His hand and know that He will feed you pure spiritual milk [His Word].

Your odds ? If you were a 500 hitter, you certainly had a winning confidence….God bats 1,000 ….He never misses a stroke! Put your confidence were the results are the surest. A good hitter watches as the ball comes toward him. If your timing isn't right your swing will reflect that. Your timing will be the difference between what you waited for and what you could actually hit. The pitcher is trying to get you out, just like satan wants us to sin.

It seemed that was when the melody of His love came into my heart, as I feasted on hearing His gentle voice in **John 10:27-30….**

"My sheep listen to my voice.

I know them, and they follow me. I give them eternal life, and they shall never perish; no one can snatch them out of my hand. My Father, who has given them to me, is greater than all; no one can snatch them out of my Father's hand. I and the Father are one.

In other words you move with the confidence you have as a hitter and use your faith with the swing. God knows the intention of our hearts, and as He see's your need for Him, He draws nearer each time you use your faith. Now get your hymnal out and sing 'Blessed Assurance' to your heavenly Father.....In Jesus Name.

Author's Insight: Babies need to learn how to walk and their mother and father always attend to their training. Would your heavenly Father do any less ? No, He stands faithfully by and according to your desires, He anxiously waits to help. Think of this verse in **Proverbs 18:10** "The name of the Lord is a strong fortress; the godly run to Him and are safe."Just think of it ! God Almighty with all His power and glory walks with us in mercy, Love and wisdom.

He can see around the corners in life that seem to blind us, and clears the hidden way. Could you, and would you trust Him completely for that. Call Him Father, call Him Son, call Him The Spirit of Truth and see how far He strays from you. He is never a breath away. And why? He is full of promises, and one of them is, "I will neither leave nor forsake you." A pretty classy person to have on your side, I'd say. Now think what his plans are for you. He will give you the best in the house, and with the fullest pay, along with a comfort, and, an unbelievable joy. Something no person can earn... it's free for trusting and obeying him. **Acknowledge Him before men and watch your blessings flow.**

Look at His credentials!

Psalm 91 (New International Version)

1. He who dwells in the shelter of the Most High
    will rest in the shadow of the Almighty.

2. I will say of the LORD, "He is my refuge and my fortress,
    my God, in whom I trust."

3. Surely he will save you from the fowler's snare
    and from the deadly pestilence.

4. He will cover you with his feathers,
    and under his wings you will find refuge;
    his faithfulness will be your shield and rampart.

5. You will not fear the terror of night,
    nor the arrow that flies by day,

6. nor the pestilence that stalks in the darkness,
    nor the plague that destroys at midday.

7. A thousand may fall at your side,
    ten thousand at your right hand,
    but it will not come near you.

8. You will only observe with your eyes
    and see the punishment of the wicked.

9. If you make the Most High your dwelling—
    even the LORD, who is my refuge-

10. Then no harm will befall you,
    no disaster will come near your tent.

11. For he will command his angels concerning you
    to guard you in all your ways;

12. They will lift you up in their hands,
    so that you will not strike your foot against a stone.

13. You will tread upon the lion and the cobra;
    you will trample the great lion and the serpent.

14. "Because he loves me," says the LORD, "I will rescue him;
    I will protect him, for he acknowledges my name.

15. He will call upon me, and I will answer him;
    I will deliver him and honor him.

16. I will be with him in trouble, With long life will I satisfy him
    and show him my salvation."

Our faith grows when we move forward in Christ

Since we believe human testimony, surely we can believe the testimony that comes from God. And God has testified about His Son. All who believe in the Son of God know that this is true. Those who don't believe this are actually calling God a liar because they don't believe what God has testified about His Son. And this is what God has testified: He has given us eternal life, and this life is in His Son. So whoever has God's Son has life; whoever does not have His Son does not have life. Final Words:

I'm writing these things to you who believe in the name of the Son of God. I'm doing it so you will know that you have eternal life. **1 John 5:9-13**

Living by Faith:

Faith is being sure of what we hope for. It is being certain of what we do not see. That is what the people of long ago were praised for. We have faith. So we understand that everything was made when God commanded it. That's why we believe that what we see was not made out of what could be seen. **Hebrew 11:1-3**

So, you see, it is impossible to please God without faith. Anyone who wants to come to Him must believe that there is a God and that He rewards those who sincerely seek Him. **Hebrews 11:6**

Is your faith growing ? If not, What stands in your way?

Isn't it time to express the hope you have inside?

Scriptures Were Written For Our Learning
Paul's Reason for Writing.

I am fully convinced, my dear brothers and sisters, that you are full of goodness. You know these things so well you can teach each other all about them.

Even so, I have been bold enough to write about some of these points, knowing that all you need is this reminder. For by God's grace, I am a special messenger from Christ Jesus to you Gentiles. I bring you the Good News so that I might present you as an acceptable offering to God, made holy by the Holy Spirit. So I have reason to be enthusiastic about all Christ Jesus has done through me in my service to God. Yet I dare not boast about anything except what Christ has done through me, bringing the Gentiles to God by my message and by the way I worked among them. They were convinced by the power of miraculous signs and wonders and by the power of God's Spirit.[i] In this way, I have fully presented the Good News of Christ from Jerusalem all the way to Illyricum.

My brothers and sisters, I am sure that you are full of goodness. What you know is complete. You are able to teach one another.

I have written to you very boldly about some things. I wanted you to think about them again. The grace of God has allowed me to serve Christ Jesus among those who aren't Jews. My duty as a priest is to preach God's good news. Then the non-Jews will become an offering that pleases God.

The Holy Spirit will make the offering holy. Because I belong to Christ Jesus, I can take pride in my work for God. I will not try to speak of anything except what Christ has done through me. He has been leading those who aren't Jews to obey God. He has been doing this by what I have said and done.

He has given me power to do signs and miracles. He has given me the power of the Holy Spirit.

From Jerusalem all the way around to Illyricum I have finished preaching the good news about Christ. I have always wanted to preach the good news where Christ was not known. I don't want to build on what someone else has started. It is written, "Those who were not told about him will understand. Those who have not heard will know what it all means."

That's why I have often been kept from coming to you. **Romans 15:14-22**

"The Apostle Paul" As The Motivation For Our Learning Continues.

Examine yourselves to see if your faith is genuine. Test yourselves. Surely you know that Jesus Christ is among you [living in you]; if not, you have failed the test of genuine faith. As you test yourselves, I hope you will recognize that we have not failed the test of apostolic authority. We pray to God that you will not do what is wrong by refusing our correction. I hope we won't need to demonstrate our authority when we arrive. Do the right thing before we come—even if that makes it look like we have failed to demonstrate our authority. For we cannot oppose the truth, but must always stand for the truth. We are glad to seem weak if it helps show that you are actually strong. We pray that you will become mature.

I am writing this to you before I come, hoping that I won't need to deal severely with you when I do come. For I want to use the authority the Lord has given me to strengthen you, not to tear you down. **(Isaiah 52:15) 2 Corinthians 13:5-9**

Paul's Final Greetings

Dear brothers and sisters, I close my letter with these last words: Be joyful. Grow to maturity. Encourage each other. Live in harmony and peace. Then the God of love and peace will be with you. Greet each other with Christian love. All of God's people here send you their greetings.

May the grace of the Lord Jesus Christ, the love of God, and the fellowship of the Holy Spirit be with you all.

Jesus Teaches about Inner Purity

Some Pharisees and teachers of religious law now arrived from Jerusalem to see Jesus. They asked him, "Why do your disciples disobey our age-old tradition? For they ignore our tradition of ceremonial hand washing before they eat." Jesus replied, "And why do you, by your traditions, violate the direct commandments of God? For instance, God says, 'Honor your father and mother,' and 'Anyone who speaks disrespectfully of father or mother must be put to death. **Matthew 15:1-4**

Dangers of the last days:

You should know this, Timothy, that in the last days there will be very difficult times. For people will love only themselves and their money. They will be boastful and proud, scoffing at God, disobedient to their parents, and ungrateful. They will consider nothing sacred. They will be unloving and unforgiving; they will slander others and have no self-control. They will be cruel and hate what is good. They will betray their friends, be reckless, be puffed up with pride, and love pleasure rather than God. They will act religious, but they will reject the power that could make them godly. Stay away from people like that! 2 Timothy 3:1-5

In John 8:31-32 Jesus said to the people who believed in him, **"You are truly my disciples if you keep obeying my teachings. And you will know the truth, and the truth will set you free."**

"Don't let your hearts be troubled. Trust in God, and trust also in me. There is more than enough room in my Father's home. If this were not so, would I have told you that I am going to prepare a place for you? When everything is ready, I will come and get you, so that you will always be with me where I am. And you know the way to where I am going." "No, we don't know, Lord," Thomas said. "We have no idea where you are going, so how can we know the way?" Jesus told him, "I am the way, the truth, and the life. No one can come to the Father except through me. If you had really known me, you would know who my Father is. From now on, you do know Him and have seen Him. **John 14:1-7**

I will pursue your commands, for you expand my understanding. **Psalm 119:32**

Blessed are you when people hate you, when they have nothing to do with you and say bad things about you, and when they treat your name as something evil. They do all this because you are followers of the Son of Man. "Their people treated the prophets the same way long ago. When these things happen to you, be glad and jump for joy. You will receive many blessings in heaven. **Luke 6:22**

Does your relationship with God bring you joy?

Or are you troubled? Does world affairs give you a growing despair? What can I do to remind myself that God is always with me? That beyond all these issues, God is still in control. Let me start you off in our search for answers.

"Do not let your hearts be troubled. Trust in God. Trust in me also.

"There are many rooms in my Father's house. If this were not true, I would have told you. I am going there to prepare a place for you. If I go and do that, I will come back. And I will take you to be with me. Then you will also be where I am. "You know the way to the place where I am going." Jesus Is the Way to the Father

Thomas said to him, "Lord, we don't know where you are going. So how can we know the way?"

Jesus answered, "I am the way and the truth and the life. No one comes to the Father except through me. If you really knew me, you would know my Father also. From now on, you do know him. And you have seen him."

"I leave my peace with you. I give my peace to you. I do not give it to you as the world does. Do not let your hearts be troubled. And do not be afraid. **John 14:1-7**

John 14:27 The joy of the Lord is your strength.

How do we keep it?

Nehemiah 8:10 & 12:43 When He gives Joy, many people hear it and are glad.

John 15:11 Where does your joy come from?

Romans 4:3 Our joy comes from knowing Jesus.

Yet we know that a man is justified or reckoned righteous and in right standing with God not by works of the Law, but only through faith and absolute reliance on and adherence to and trust in Jesus Christ, the Messiah, the Anointed One. Therefore, even we ourselves have believed on Christ Jesus, in order to be justified by faith in Christ and not by works of the Law, for we cannot be justified by any observance of the ritual of the Law given by Moses, because by keeping legal rituals and by works no human being can ever be justified, declared righteous and put in right standing with God.

But if, in our desire and endeavor to be justified in Christ, to be declared righteous and put in right standing with God wholly and solely through Christ, we have shown ourselves sinners also and convicted of sin, does that make Christ a minister.....a party and contributor to our sin?..... Banish the thought! Of course not!

Galatians 2:17-19

For if I, or any others who have taught that the observance of the Law of Moses is not essential to being justified by God should now by word or practice teach or intimate that it is essential to, build up again what I tore down, I prove myself a transgressor.

For I through the Law, under the operation of the curse of the Law, have in Christ's death for me, myself died to the Law and all the Law's demands upon me, so that I may, henceforth, live to and for God.

I have been crucified with Christ, in Him I have shared His crucifixion; it is no longer I who live, but Christ, the Messiah lives in me; and the life I now live in the body I live by faith in, by adherence to and reliance on and complete trust in the Son of God, Who loved me and gave Himself up for me.

Therefore, I do not treat God's gracious gift as something of minor importance and defeat its very purpose; I do not set aside and invalidate and frustrate and nullify the grace, unmerited favor of God. For if justification, righteousness, acquittal from guilt, comes through observing the ritual of the Law, then Christ the Messiah died groundlessly and to no purpose and in vain. His death was then wholly superfluous.

Galatians 2:16-21

In all of scripture, after I made a commitment to Him, I haven't identified myself more with Christ than these verses above. They are a large part of the nourishment that sustains me in the truth of my every day existence with Him in this world. It's like, how and why does a heart pump without a body. He is truly a life, for life and hope to all His children. How is a body moved without a heart? Are you thirsty?.....You need more of the Holy Spirit. Real joy with a tender longing, combined with love for Jesus and your neighbor.

Living the Chosen Life as Studied

In Him was life, and that life was the light of men. **John 1:4**

You have a life, give it to Him. We are only clay. He molds us and makes us into the beauty He created us for. Did you stop His molding years ago? He can still finish it, for nothing is impossible with God. **Luke 1:37**

He was in the world, and though the world was made through Him, the world did not recognize Him. He came to that which was his own, but his own did not receive Him. Yet to all who received Him, to those who believed in His name, He gave the right to become children of God—children born not of natural descent, nor of human decision or a husband's will, but born of God. **John 1:10–13**

Receiving Him brings a powerful flow of love and commitment to the believer Even the devil believes and trembles. **James 2:19**

This is a compliment to the path we have chosen in **John 3:3. You must be born again!** It is the thrust behind A Chosen Life Study! Without the Holy Spirit there would be no reason for this book.

Do you think of yourself as a 'chosen' person? If we are really honest and look at the world around us, it is difficult to feel like a chosen person. The main reason I labeled this for discussion is to look at the work that Jesus has done for all of us. Being a chosen one are words that He has given us. They are meant to tell us that He has set us apart from the rest of the world. We no longer act, feel, or operate our lives as worldly people. Instead, we have His life, His name and His Spirit inside of us. We can't see it, but we have certainly felt it, and loved it from the first awareness. We keep reaching out for Him with the tenderness that He has given us. And so, with that process our lives have changed according to the grace, strength and faith He is renewing us with.

Accordingly, each of us are different, but certainly appreciate that the arm needs the fingers; and the fingers need the toes.

For this Blessing:

What does God mean when He declares:

"But you are a chosen people, a royal priesthood, a Holy Nation, a people belonging to God, that you may **'declare the praises of Him'** *who called you out of darkness into His marvelous light"?* **1 Peter 2:9**

Repeat the phrase **'declare the praises of Him'** To yourself, to see if you hear the voice of the Son of man.

And This Blessing:

He taught me how to fish for men when He **said 'follow me, son.'** So, with a hunger for the bible, I read it daily. It is food for your heart and body.

No one ever understands these verses completely until he or she has been redeemed by the Blood of the Lamb. Many go through life not caring enough to find out where they stand in the light of eternal blessings and rewards. They are stored up for all who take the time to look for the God of their salvation and reach out for the hand of His Son, who died in their place that they might truly live for His glory.

I remember sitting on the bench at football games, hoping to be 'chosen' so I could be involved with the game. If the coach would only call my name, I thought. Then what happiness I experienced when I heard him call my name in front of all the other players. In reality he was saying, "You are now a part of this game." Excited, I would run on to the field with instructions for the team. But, most importantly, I had a chance to participate in the action. I had been chosen to do the things my heart desired. Is that what God Almighty is saying He wants of us to come in to His Kingdom?

My membership on that high school football team ended when I graduated. But I was enrolled in the family of God by His grace, and was given a never-ending membership because I believed the story He told me. His promise to me is, "I will neither leave you or forsake you." Think of it! He called me off the bench of life and made me a participant. I hadn't yet practiced for a single day, yet He let me participate! He shows me things to do and people to love. No wonder, as He speaks to me, I always feel like a member of His team, and the ball I now carry is the Word of God, and my headgear is the Helmet of Salvation (see Ephesians 6:17). He promises "team membership" to "all who received Him. To those who believed in His name, He gave them the right to be children of God" **John 1:12**

Being a part of the chosen life is available to people of all ages. God does not choose us on the basis of our past, present, or things we have or have not done.

"For God so loved the world that He gave us His One and Only Son, that whoever believes in Him shall not perish but have eternal life." **John 3:16.**

His one requirement is faith: Like a balloon, it blows up higher and higher and higher until it bursts through the gates of heaven into the arms of Jesus; Glorifying the Spirit of God who loves us and carries us home.

Without faith it isn't possible to please God. Those who come to God must believe that he exists. And they must believe that he rewards those who look to him

Hebrews 11:6

For it is by grace you have been saved, through faith—and this is not from yourselves, it is the gift of God—not by works, so that no one can boast.

Ephesians 2:8–9

God's grace has saved you because of your faith in Christ. Your salvation doesn't come from anything you do. It is God's gift. Since it is not based on anything we have done. No one can brag about earning it.

The Test of Jesus in you: Study these bible verses and see what God is seeking in you. That is where the word study comes from in the title of this book, A Chosen Life Study.

Examine yourselves too see whether you are in the faith; Test yourselves. Do you not realize that Christ Jesus is in you…..Unless of course, you fail

2 Corinthians 13:5

Seriously, I need His presence in my life everyday that I live in this body, according to my own experiences with Him, and as told to us in **1 Peter 2:9**

Can being Chosen By God bring excitement to Your Life? Check out these verses:

And do the verses below have a common thread.

John 3:3-5 God's special gift of love and salvation is immeasurable.

2 Corinthians 5:17 A new and wonderfully exciting life has invaded your life.

Revelation 3:19-20 He knocks, asking you to open the door to your heart. Let Him in.

Ezekiel 11:19 & 18:31 And certainly one to remember is **18:31**

(Ezekiel 18:31) Rid yourselves of all the offenses you have committed, and get a new heart and a new spirit. Why will you die, house of Israel? ³² For I take no pleasure in the death of anyone, declares the Sovereign LORD. Repent and live!)

Jeremiah 31:31-35 See if all of these speak to you. Are You Thirsty? If not you may still need to quench your thirst in Jesus.

"Wash yourselves and be clean! Let me no longer see your evil deeds. Give up your wicked ways. Learn to do good. Seek justice. Help the oppressed. Defend the orphan. Fight for the rights of widows.

"Come now, let us argue this out," says the LORD. "No matter how deep the stain of your sins, I can remove it. I can make you as clean as freshly fallen snow. Even if you are stained as red as crimson, I can make you as white as wool. If you will only obey me and let me help you, then you will have plenty to eat. But if you keep turning away and refusing to listen, you will be destroyed by your enemies. I, the LORD, have spoken!"   **Isaiah 1:16–20**

To everyone who is thirsty, He says, Come!

Jesus has water that will quench your thirst and wash you clean.

"Come,"

All of you who are thirsty, come to the waters; Come to Jesus. **Spirit And Truth.**

And you who have no money, come buy and eat! Come, buy wine and milk without money and without cost. Why spend money on what is not bread, and your labor on what does not satisfy? Listen, listen to me, and eat what is good, and your soul will delight in the richest of fare. Give ear and come to me; hear me that your soul may live. I will make an everlasting covenant with you, my faithful love promised to David. See, I have made him a witness to the peoples, a leader and commander of the peoples. Surely you will summon nations you know not, and nations that do not know you will hasten to you, because of the Lord your God, the Holy One of Israel, for He has endowed you with splendor."

Seek the Lord while he may be found; call on Him while He is near. Let the wicked forsake his way and the evil man his thoughts. Let him turn to the Lord, and He will have mercy on him, and to our God, for He will freely pardon. "For your thoughts are not my thoughts, neither are your ways my ways," declares the Lord. "As the heavens are higher than the earth, so are my ways higher than yours and my thoughts than your thoughts. As the rain and the snow come down from heaven, and do not return to it without watering the earth and making it bud and flourish, so that it yields seed for the sower and bread for the eater, so is my word that goes out from my mouth: It will not return to me empty, but will accomplish what I desire and achieve the purpose for which I sent it "You will go out in joy and be led forth in peace; the mountains and hills will burst into song before you, and all the trees of the field will clap their hands. Instead of the thorn bush will grow the pine tree, and instead of briers the myrtle will grow. This will, be for the Lord's renown, for an everlasting sign, which will not be destroyed." **Isaiah 55:1–15**

He will rain down on you. And His voice will not return before He has loved you to Him; watered you with His Spirit. For God is love. God's Word Sets Us Free

Analyze…And, memorize All the following verses

And then tuck them into your heart.

Place them in your heart in a way that you would put furniture in a room. Take all of them, they are an adorning and everything has a place and a purpose with one difference. You can't move them around so they present a different look or satisfy your purpose better. They are solid like a rock to stand on; and for that reason I placed a box below. We must go to the Son who wrote the bible. That is our home forever, as recorded in Mark.

In the same way, when you see all these things taking place, you can know that His return is very near, right at the door. I tell you the truth, this generation will not pass from the scene before all these things take place. Heaven and earth will disappear, but my words will never disappear. **Mark 13:29-31**

Studying the Scriptures, with Jesus living in our hearts gives, brings, and allows us His power as it helps us to understand how to live a life free from the habit of sinning sin. Set aside, being chosen. Like a waiting bride, as He gives us daily instructions from His word.

Long ago God spoke many times and in many places to our ancestors through the prophets. The Son reflects God's own glory, and everything about Him represents God exactly. He sustains the universe by the mighty power of His command. After He died to cleanse us from the stain of sin, He sat down in the place of honor at the right of the majestic God in heaven. **Hebrews 1: 1–3**

All Scripture is inspired by God and is useful to teach us what is true and to make us realize what is wrong in our lives. It straightens us out and teaches us to do what is right. It is God's way of preparing us in every way, fully equipped for every good thing God wants us to do. **2 Timothy 3:16-17**

Jesus told him, "I am the way, the truth, and the life. No one can come to the Father except through me. If you had known who I am, then you would have known who my Father is. now on you know him and have seen him!" **John 16:6-7**

Later, when Jesus was alone with the twelve disciples and with the others who were gathered around, they asked him, "What do your stories mean?" He replied, "You are permitted to understand the secret about the Kingdom of God. But I am using these stories to conceal everything about it from outsiders, so that the Scriptures might be fulfilled. **Mark 4:10-12**

Then Jesus asked them, "Would anyone light a lamp and then put it under a basket or under a bed to shut out the light? Of course not! A lamp is placed on a stand, where its light will shine. "Everything that is now hidden or secret will eventually be brought to light. Anyone who is willing to hear should listen and understand! And be sure to pay attention to what you hear. The more you do this, the more you will understand—and even more, besides. To those who are open to my teaching, more understanding will be given. But to those who are not listening, even what they have will be taken away from them." **Mark 4:21–25**

I am the one who corrects and disciplines everyone I love. Be diligent and turn from your indifference. "Look! Here I stand at the door and knock. If you hear me calling and open the door, I will come in, and we will share a meal as friends."

Revelation 3:19–20

They offer superficial treatments for my people's mortal wound. They give assurances of peace when all is war. Are they ashamed when they do these disgusting things? No, not at all—they don't even blush!

They bandage the wounds of my people
as if they were not very deep. 'Peace, peace,' they say.
But there isn't any peace. Are they ashamed of their hateful actions?
No. They do not feel any shame at all.
They do not even know how to blush.
So they will fall like others who have already fallen.
They will be brought down when I punish them," says the Lord. **Jeremiah 6:14-15**

To whom can I give warning? Who will listen when I speak?

Their ears are closed, and they cannot hear. They scorn the Word of the Lord. They don't want to listen at all. So now I am filled with the Lord's fury.

Yes, I am weary of holding it in! "I will pour out my fury over Jerusalem, even on children playing in the streets, on gatherings of young men, and on husbands and wives and grandparents." **Jeremiah 6:10–11**

Sinners will be killed by their own evil. The enemies of godly people will be judged. The Lord sets those who serve him free. No one who goes to him for safety will be judged. **Psalm 34:21-22**

When a person who is accountable hasn't received Jesus into their life they are walking alone without God, and it is my belief they soon become wicked, or straying. It is so dangerous in many ways as no one knows when His return will be. People are in a continuous mode forever, without Jesus in their hearts. This box graciously included because *He uses the word wicked* so many times in His word.

This text brought back to you for careful consideration. Place this along side of the verse in **2 Corinthians 13:5,** and then praise God with a new heart.

They have healed also the wound of the daughter of My people lightly and neglectfully, saying, Peace, peace, when there is no peace. Were they brought to shame because they had committed abominations. Extremely disgusting and vile things? No, they were not at all ashamed, nor could they blush [at their idolatry. Therefore they shall fall among those who fall; at the time that I punish them they shall be overthrown, says the Lord. **Jeremiah 6:14-15**

I love to Tell the Story

A. Catherine Hankey, 1834-1911   William G. Fischer 1835-1912

1. I love to tell the sto - ry   Of un – seen things a – above, Of
   Je – sus and His glo – ry,   Of Je – sus and His love; I love to
   Tell the sto – ry Be-cause I know 'tis   true, It sat – is – fies   my
   Long – ings As noth – ing else can do. I love to tell the sto – ry!
'Twill be my theme in glo-ry- To tell the Old, Old sto-ry Of Je-sus and His love.

2. I love to tell the sto – ry - More won – der – ful it seems   Than
   All gold – en fan – cies   Of all our gold – en dreams; I love to
   Tell the sto – ry - It did so much for me, And that is just the
   Rea – son I tell it now to thee. I love to tell the sto – ry!
'Twill be my theme in glo-ry- To tell the Old, Old sto-ry Of Je-sus and His love.

3. I love to tell the sto – ry - 'Tis   pleas – ant to re – peat   What
   Seems, each time I tell it, more won – der - ly sweet; I love to
   Tell the sto – ry For some have nev – er heard   The mes – sage of sal –
   Va - tion   from God's own ho – ly Word. I love to tell the sto – ry!
'Twill be my theme in glo-ry- To tell the Old, Old sto-ry Of Je-sus and His love.

4. I love to tell the sto – ry , For those who know it best   Seem
   Hun – nger – ing and thirst – ing To hear it like the rest; And when in
   Scenes of glo – ry I sing the new, new song, 'Twill be the old, old
   Sto – ry That I have loved so long. I love to tell the sto – ry!
'Twill be my theme in glo-ry- To tell the Old, Old sto-ry Of Je-sus and His love.

There Is Hope In Jesus; Our only Messiah; For Everyone!

My Children, forget not my law;

But let thine heart keep my

Commandments: For length of days,

And long life, and peace, shall they

Add to thee. Let not mercy and truth

Forsake thee: bind them about thy neck;

Write them upon the tablet of thine heart:

So shalt thou find favor and good

Understanding in the sight of God and man.

Trust in the Lord with all thine heart:

And lean not unto thine understanding.

In all thy ways acknowledge Him,

And He shall direct thy paths. **Proverbs 3:1-6**

His light always shines and the darkness can't put it out because He is the light of the world. The clip above and below are truly salutations to His character and name. I love His words, all of them. They are my light and hope. I long to have Him speak to me, **at this books ending in John 17** where Jesus prayed for me. I am going to make it…me and my family. We have Jesus!

Nevertheless, that time of darkness and despair will not go on forever. The land of Zebulun and Naphtali will soon be humbled, but there will be a time in the future when Galilee of the Gentiles, which lies along the road that runs between the Jordan and the sea, will be filled with glory. The people who walk in darkness will see a great light–a light that will shine on all who live in the land where death casts its shadow. Israel will again be great, and its people will rejoice as people rejoice at harvest time. They will shout with joy like warriors dividing the plunder. For God will break the chains that bind His people and the whip that scourges them, just as He did when he destroyed the army of Midian with Gideon's little band. In that day of peace, battle gear will no longer be issued. Never again will uniforms be bloodstained by war. All such equipment will be burned.

For a child is born to us, a son is given to us. And the government will rest on His shoulders. These will be His royal titles: Wonderful Counselor, Mighty God, Everlasting Father, Prince of Peace. His ever expanding, peaceful government will never end. He will rule forever with fairness and justice from the throne of His ancestor David. The passionate commitment of the Lord Almighty will guarantee this!

Isaiah 9:1-7

Can you remember a time when God Almighty has brought you through a time of darkness and despair? What was your response?

Our Awesome God:

Lord, You Have Established My Way

O Lord, you have examined my heart,

And know everything about me.

You know when I sit down or stand up.

You know my every thought when far away.

You chart the path ahead of me

And tell me where to stop and rest.

Every moment you know where I am.

You know what I am going to say, even before I say it, LORD.

You both precede and follow me.

You place your hand of blessing upon my head.

Such knowledge is too wonderful for me,

Too great for me to know!

I can never escape from your spirit!

I can never get away from your presence!

If I go up to Heaven, you are there;

If I go down to the place of the dead, you are there.

If I ride the wings of the morning,

If I dwell by the farthest oceans,

Even there your hand will guide me,

and your strength will support me. **Psalm 139:1-10**

You, O Lord, Have Put a New Song In My Mouth

A Hymn of Praise to Our God

I could ask the darkness to hide me,

And the light around me to become night–

but even in darkness I cannot hide from you.

To You the night shines as bright as day.

Darkness and light are both alike to you.

You made all the delicate inner parts of my body

And knit me together in my mother's womb.

Thank you for making me so wonderfully complex.

Your workmanship is marvelous–and how well I know it.

You watched me as I was being formed in utter seclusion,

As I was woven together in the dark of the womb. You saw me before I was born.

Every day of my life was recorded in your book.

Every moment was laid out before a single day had passed.

How precious are your thoughts about me, O God! They are innumerable!

I can't even count them! They outnumber the grains of the sand. **Ps. 139:11–18**

And when I wake up in the morning, you are still with me.

Psalm 17:14

Recognizing His Voice?

His Word will speak to you!

"This New Life Is A "Mystery" Some people turn it down; Others run to it.

Proverbs 18:10 The name of the Lord is like a strong tower.
 Godly people run to Him and are safe..

This new life hidden in Christ, is the truth of our faith, and it is the mystery of Godliness. My old self has been crucified with Christ. It is no longer I who live, but Christ who lives in me. So I live in this earthly body by trusting in the Son of God, who loved me and gave himself for me.

In this short hymn, Paul affirms the humanity and divinity of Christ. By so doing he reveals the heart of the good news "The great mystery of our faith" (the secret of how we become godly). "Appeared in the flesh"—Jesus was a man; Jesus' incarnation is the basis of our being right with God. "Was shown to be righteous the Spirit."—Jesus' resurrection showed that the Holy Spirit's power was in Him. 'Was seen by angels' and 'was taken up into heaven'—Jesus is divine. We can't please God on our own; we must depend on Christ.

As a man, Jesus lived a perfect life, and so he is a perfect example of how to live. As God, Jesus gives us the power to do what is right. It is possible to live A godly life through following Christ. **Commentary on Galatians 2:20**

I correct and discipline everyone I love. So be diligent and turn from your indifference. Look, Bob! I stand at the door and knock. If you hear my voice and open the door, I will come in, and we will share a meal together as friends. Those who are victorious will sit with me on my throne, just as I was victorious and sat with my Father on his throne.

Anyone with ears to hear must listen to the Spirit and understand what he is saying to the churches. **Revelations 3: 19-22**

When we receive this new life in Christ, our life has been fulfilled by God's plan for our lives and we become His ambassadors to our world.

Whatever we do, it is because Christ's love controls us. Since we believe that Christ died for everyone, we also believe that we have all died to the old life we used to live. He died for everyone so that those who receive his new life will no longer live to please themselves. Instead they will live to please Christ, who died and was raised for them. So we have stopped evaluating others by what the world thinks about them. Once I mistakenly thought of Christ that way, as though he was merely a human being. How differently I think about Him now!

What this means is that those who become Christians become new persons. They are not the same anymore, for the old life is gone. A new life has begun! All this newness of life is from God, who brought us back to Himself through what Christ did. And God has given us the task of reconciling people to Him. For God was in Christ, reconciling the world to Himself, no longer counting people's sins against them. This is the wonderful message He has given us to tell others. We are Christ's ambassadors, and God is using us to speak to you. We urge you, as though Christ Himself were here pleading with you. "Be reconciled to God!" For God made Christ, who never sinned, to be the offering for your sins, so that we could be made right with God through Christ. As God's partners, we beg you not to reject this marvelous message of God's great kindness.

For God says: "At just the right time, I heard you. On the day of salvation, I helped you." Indeed, God is ready to help you right now. Today is the day of salvation.

1Corinthians 5:14–6:2

Jesus called out to me, "Come, follow me, Bob, and I will show you how to fish for people!" **Matthew 4:19**

Why do I want you to know Jesus? With His Word He helped me in this matter 35 years ago with a surgery on my heart…..He is calling you through His word; as you read in a Chosen Life Study. He sees your face and I know His heart. He tells me that your face and heart will shine for Him in heaven on your appointed day, By believing and trusting in Jesus. Of course, I have no need of human witnesses, but I say these things so you might be saved. **John 5:34**

He will tell you how you and everyone in your household can be saved. **Acts 11:14**

A Chosen Life Study

Is God's power evidenced in your life? There are additional scriptures that speak of a new life where the old is gone and a new life begins…can you think of others besides these few that are listed. People are usually excited when they experience Jesus living in them, because they have joined the ranks of an unbelievable group. They are elected and set apart for Jesus

Jeremiah 29: 11-14 Jeremiah say's that **God** has plans for us.

John 10:10 "The thief!" Is he holding you back?

John 14:6&7 But the Lord's plans: Are always brighter and better.

There is a battle going on in this world that the human eye cannot see….It is Spiritual….. Christians are doing battle with Satan to gain others for Christ. Are you standing with Christ, Because the battle belongs to the Lord.

He does however, enlist our help. Are your sleeves rolled up from your wrists to your shoulders?

When you come face to face with Jesus Christ you will understand why you need Him.

There is always a before and after: It takes place with new believers when **His** new life begins.

1 Peter 2:10 Explains: Once you were not a people. But now you are the people of God. Once you had not received mercy. But now you have received mercy. Dear friends, you are outsiders and strangers in this world. So I'm asking you not to give in to your sinful longings. They fight against your soul. People who don't believe might say you are doing wrong. But lead good lives among them. Then they will see your good works. And they will give glory to God on the day he comes to judge.

Does the above tell you this: I was only flesh and bones with no heart to see Jesus. Then Jesus saw me naked and blind, and in need of nourishment for my spirit. He added food (His Word) for my bones, and the Good News for eyes that can see Jesus. Now He sees my heart and fills it for Himself and others. I found new friends in His Kingdom that He was keeping just for my spiritual nourishment, and growth. Now I have grown to know Jesus, the King of Kings, and Lord of Lords, with a nourishment from Christ that I can share with other people so they too can grow in the Spirit and know Jesus. It was all free for myself and all those that He call's to be His very own.

'Oh Sweet Jesus!' Our one and only Savior.'
King Of Kings And Lord Of Lords. Rev. 19:16
I Am Alpha and Omega,
The Beginning And The End. Rev. 1:8
Wonderful Counselor, Mighty God,
Everlasting Father,
Prince Of Peace. Isaiah 9:6

In Him Was Life,

And That Life Was The Light Of Men. John 1:4

But very truly I tell you, it is for your good that I am going away. Unless I go away, the
Advocate (Spirit) will not come to you; but if I go, I will send him to you. John 16:7

Chapter Five

Here Is our Hope In The Messiah

God Our Father, Creator,

Gave us His Saving Son

With The

Counseling Holy Spirit's Power And Presence.

From a jack to a King, While looking back on chapter 4: The blessedness of Jesus in His Reincarnation. While gaining wisdom and knowledge regarding these three points: a. It reveals Grace and Joy for the believer. B. The secret of how we become Godly. C. Jesus was divine. We cannot please God on our own. We must depend on Christ.

We are the jack, He is the King. The basics: 1. Search your heart for Christ. Pg 80 He is our light and life. 2. Have you really met Jesus? Pgs 77-81 3. Are you been born of the Holy Spirit? 4. And are you moving forward with Christ? P-90-93 5. Are you learning, & growing with inner purity? 6. Do you pursue Him through His word? P-93-98 7. Are you thirsting for more of Jesus? God's word sets us free. Do you feel free from your sins? p 92-94. God is awesome=His word will speak to you. 8. The new life is a mystery—are you a part of that mystery? 9. If you are immersed in His word, is it evidenced in your life? P 92-(95)-102 'Onward Christian Soldier.'

Christ is the Head of the Church, which is His Body. He is the first of all who will rise from the dead, so He is first in everything. For God in all his fullness was pleased to live in Christ, and by Him God reconciled everything to Himself.

He made peace with everything in heaven and on earth by means of His Blood on the cross. **Colossians 1:15 & 20**

The Trinity

Father

"Ah, Sovereign Lord, you have made the heavens and the earth by your great power and outstretched arm. Nothing is too hard for you. You show love to thousands but bring the punishment for the fathers' sins into the laps of their children after them. O great and Powerful God, whose name is the Lord Almighty, great are your purposes and mighty are your deeds. Your eyes are open to all the ways of men; you reward everyone according to his conduct and as his deeds deserve.

Son

For unto us a child is born, to us a Son is given, and the government will be upon His shoulders. And He will be called Wonderful Counselor, Mighty God, Everlasting Father, Prince of Peace. **Isaiah 9:6**

Holy Spirit

"But you will receive power when the Holy Spirit comes on you. Then you will be my witnesses in Jerusalem. You will be my witnesses in all Judea and Samaria. And you will be my witnesses from one end of the earth to the other." Be my witnesses from one end of the earth to the other." **Acts 1:8**

In the last days, God says, "I will pour out my Spirit on all people." This is the word of the Lord to Zerubbabel: "Not by might, nor by power, but by my Spirit," says the Lord Almighty. **Zechariah 4:6**

Three in One:

Revelation 4:8a we read: "Holy, Holy, Holy is the Lord God Almighty, who was, and is, and is to come."

He came into the very world He created, but the world didn't recognize Him. He came to his own people, and even they rejected Him. But to all who believed Him and accepted Him, He gave the right to become children of God. They are reborn—not with a physical birth resulting from human passion or plan, but a birth that comes from God. So the Word became human and made His home among us. He was full of unfailing love and faithfulness. And we have seen His glory, the glory of the Father's One and Only Son. **John 1:10-14**

According to God's own word, He was pleased to live in Christ, representing the Church which he established by His own blood. He is the first and the last of all, in everything that has been created. There is nothing in all creation that wasn't created and established through Christ. He is all and all. **Colossians 1:19-22**

That light is Jesus! Have you invited Him into your precious heart, empowering you to receive His power and commands? It is the resurrection power. Everyone needs Him in order to be born again…New life while your sins are nailed to the cross. Gone. As far away as the east is from the West, He will remember them no more. Jesus own statement, and word to all of us.

Does that alone bring joy to your heart. That is His design, and to see how we handle it. No matter what other happiness I have in this world, He fulfills it. Reread the two bible verses above.

'Light'

Christians are 'More Than Conquerors' Romans 8:7

I create the light and make the darkness. I send good times and bad

times. I, the Lord, am the one who does these things. **Isaiah 45:7**

I Bob, lived in darkness until, by invitation, He came into my life…For without Christ there is only darkness. No direction and consequently no Godly purpose.

The name of the Lord is a strong fortress the Godly run to Him and are safe.

The rich think of their wealth as a strong defense; they imagine it to be a high wall of safety. **Proverbs 18:10-11**

But the poor realize there are two kinds of perfection which the Christian needs. *I had no striving until I met Jesus.* First, the perfection of justification in Christ. Second, the perfection of sanctification wrought in him by the Holy Spirit and given to us freely by the Spirit, His word and fellowship with other believers. These choices every believer should strive for.

Romans 8:37-39 No, despite all these things, we are more than 'conquerors,' and the victory is ours through Christ, who loved us. And I am convinced that nothing can ever separate us from God's love. Neither death nor life, neither angels nor demons, neither our fears for today nor our worries about tomorrow—not even the powers of hell can separate us from God's love. No power in the sky above or in the earth below—indeed, nothing in all creation will ever be able to separate us from the love of God that is revealed in Christ Jesus our Lord.

Holy, Holy, Holy
Nicaea

Reginald Heber, 1783-1826   John B. Dykes, 1823-1876

Ho – ly, Ho – ly, Ho – ly, Lord God Al – might – y! Ear – ly in the
Morn – ing our song shall rise to Thee;   Ho – ly, Ho – ly, Ho – ly!
Mer – ci – ful and Might – y!   God in Three Per – sons, bless – ed Trin – i – ty

Ho – ly, Ho – ly, Ho – ly ! All the saints a – dore Thee, Cast – ing down their
Gold – en crowns a – round the glass – y sea;   Cher – u – bim and ser – a – phim
Fall – ing down be – fore Thee, Which wert and art and ev – er – more shalt be.

Ho – ly, Ho – ly, Ho – ly ! Tho the dark – ness hide Thee, Tho the eye of
Sin – ful man Thy glo – ry may not see;   On – ly Thou art ho – ly –
There is none be – side Thee Per – fect in pow'r , in love and pur – i – ty.

Ho – ly, Ho – ly, Ho – ly, Lord God Al – mighty – y! All Thy works shall
Praise Thy name in earth and sky and sea; Ho – ly, Ho – ly, Ho – ly!
Mer – ci – ful and Might – y! God in Three Per – sons, bless – ed Trin – i – ty!

Athanasius…Patriarch of Alexandria…championed the definition of the Christian faith accepted at Nicaea in the Arian controversy (*Aryanism)

The Athanasius Creed

Unless a man accept and believeth this faith; without a doubt he shall perish everlastingly. And the Universal faith is this:

That we worship one God in Trinity, and Trinity in Unity; Neither confounding the persons nor dividing the substance. For there is one person of the Father, another of the Son, and another of the Holy Spirit. But the Godhead of the Father, of the

Son, and of the Holy Spirit is all one, the glory equal, the majesty coeternal.

Such as the Father is, such is the Son, and such is the Holy Spirit. The Father uncreated, the Son uncreated, and the Holy Spirit uncreated. The Father incomprehensible, the Son incomprehensible, and the Holy Spirit incomprehensible. The Father eternal, the Son eternal, and the Holy Spirit eternal. And yet there are not three eternals, but one eternal. As also there are

not three uncreated nor three incomprehensible, but one uncreated and one incomprehensible. So likewise the Father is almighty, the Son almighty, and the Holy Spirit is almighty. And yet there are not three almighty's, but one almighty

So the Father is God, the Son is God, and the Holy Spirit is God; And yet there are not three Gods but one God.

So likewise the Father is Lord, the Son Lord, and the Holy Spirit Lord; And yet

not three Lords, but one Lord. For like as we are compelled by the Christian and Lord; So we are forbidden by the universal religion to say, there are three Gods or

three Lords. The Father is made of none, neither created nor begotten.

The Son is of the Father alone; not made nor created, but begotten. The Holy Spirit is of the Father and of the Son, neither made, nor created, nor begotten, but proceeding. So there is one Father, not three Fathers; one Son,

not three Sons; one Holy Spirit, not three Holy Spirits. And in this Trinity none is afore or after another; none is greater or less than another. But the whole three Persons are

coeternal, and coequal. So that in all things, as foresaid, the Unity in the Trinity

and the Trinity in Unity is to be worshipped. He therefore that will be saved must

thus think of the Trinity. Furthermore, it is necessary to everlasting salvation

that he also believe faithfully in the incarnation of our Lord Jesus Christ. For the

right faith is that we believe and confess that our Lord Jesus Christ, the Son of God, is God and man. God of the substance of the Father,

begotten before all worlds; and man of the substance of His mother, born in the world. Perfect God and perfect man, of a reasonable soul and human flesh subsisting. Equal to the Father as touching His Godhead and inferior to the Father as touching His manhood. Who, although He is God and man, yet He is not two, but one Christ. One, not by conversion of the Godhead into flesh, but taking of that manhood into God. One altogether, not by confusion of substance, but by unity of person.

For as the reasonable soul and flesh are one man, so God and man are one in Christ;

Who suffered for our salvation, descended into hell, rose again the third day from

the dead; He ascended into heaven; He sits on the right hand of the Father, God

Almighty; From whence he shall come to judge the quick and the dead.

At whose coming all men shall rise again with their bodies, and shall

give an account of their own works. And they that have done good

shall go into life everlasting, and they that have done evil into everlasting fire. **This is the universal faith, which except a man believe faithfully, he cannot be saved.**

Father, Son, And Holy Spirit

Who can explain the Trinity, who can know of His plan?

Who can approach the throne of God, or walk with Him hand in hand...

The answer lies in 'The Word Of God,' by faith He calls us His own,

His light has shown on the Father and Son, bringing hope in the Spirit alone...

He calls us with haste to His Word, 'Come' on wings of the 'Dove'

With wisdom and power the Spirit will lead; Yeah, 'Come' as He whispers His love...

The Spirit points to the Fortress on high;

In the strength of his name, on wings you will fly...

To the God of power and Grace,

You come to His love, and His mercy embrace...

To be home with the Lord of the Nations, United again with His own... Blessed are you in His bosom,

To be near Him, and never alone... **Poem by Bob Bowman**

He is God and God alone. When Moses ask Him, "Who shall I say sent me" His response was, Tell them "I am sent you." ... Jesus said many times that He is "I Am" As in "I am the resurrection and the life." ... "I am the light of the world." ... I am the way the truth and the life." "I am your God, saith the Lord God," Ezekiel 34:31.

O. K memory folks! Rest and remember each place separated by a dots. Say it to yourself for a week, or however. Then put the beautiful expression together as you are able, by checking it often for His glory and your memory.

Honor and Serve the Lord according to His Triune plan.

God desires to live in your heart. When you give your whole heart to God, it is evidenced in your entire life.

"So honor the Lord and serve Him wholeheartedly. Put away forever the idols your ancestors worshiped when they lived beyond the Euphrates River and in Egypt. Serve the Lord alone. But if you are unwilling to serve the Lord, then choose today whom you will serve. Would you prefer the gods your ancestors served beyond the Euphrates? Or will it be the gods of the

Amorites in whose land you now live? But as for me and my family, we will serve the Lord." The people replied, "We would never forsake the Lord. and worship other gods. For the Lord our God is the one who rescued us and our ancestors from slavery in the land of Egypt. He performed mighty miracles before our very eyes. As we traveled through the wilderness among our enemies, He preserved us. It was the Lord who drove out the Amorites and the other nations living here in the land. So we, too, will serve the Lord, for he alone is our God."

Then Joshua said to the people, "You are not able to serve the Lord, for He is a Holy and jealous God. He will not forgive your rebellion and sins. If you forsake the Lord and serve other gods, He will turn against you and destroy you, even though He has been so good to you."

But the people answered Joshua, saying, "No, we are determined to serve the Lord!" "You are accountable for this decision," Joshua said. "You have chosen to serve the Lord." "Yes," they replied, "we are accountable." "All right then," Joshua said, "destroy the idols among you, and turn your hearts

to the Lord, the God of Israel." The people said to Joshua, "We will serve the Lord our God. We will obey Him alone." So Joshua made a covenant with the people that day at Shechem, committing them to a permanent and binding contract between themselves and the Lord.

Joshua recorded these things in the Book of the Law of God. As a reminder of their agreement, he took a huge stone and rolled it beneath the oak tree beside the Tabernacle of the Lord. Joshua said to all the people, "This stone has heard everything the Lord said to us. It will be a witness to testify against you if you go back on your word to God.' Then Joshua sent the people away, each to his own inheritance. **Joshua 24:14–28**

Record your prayerful response to this scripture passage in Joshua 24:14-28

Example:

1. What other Gods do people serve in our days? Are there God's lurking around in anyone's life to be exposed and let go of?

2. How can we respect and respond to His Holiness?

3. Are broken promises or commitments on our part the end of the line, revealing our failure, or is their still hope?

4. Thanksgiving and prayers for friends….

5. To Love Them in our prayer life.

6. Praises For Our Living God and Savior?

Read Romans 3:23-24 then, Romans 6:20-23

Other :

So God can point to us in all future ages as examples of the incredible wealth of His grace and kindness toward us, as shown in all He has done for us who are united with Christ Jesus.

God saved you by His grace when you believed. And you can't take credit for this; it is a gift from God. Salvation is not a reward for the good things we have done, so none of us can boast about it. For we are God's masterpiece. He has created us anew in Christ Jesus, so we can do the good things He planned for us long ago. **Ephesians 2:7-10**

Oneness and Peace with and in Christ ....Yes we remember His love endures, even today?

Christ Is Supreme In All Things

Jesus Christ has authority over everything on Earth. Christ is the visible image of the invisible God. He existed before God made anything at all and is supreme over all creation. Christ is the one through whom God create everything in heaven and earth. He made the things we can see and the things we can't see–kings, kingdoms, rulers, and authorities. Everything has been created through Him and for Him. He existed before everything else began, and He holds all creation together. Christ is the head of His Church, which is His body. He is the first of all who will rise from the dead, so He is first in everything. For God in all His fullness was pleased to live in Christ, and by Him God reconciled everything to Himself. He made peace with everything in heaven and on earth by means of His Blood on the cross.
Colossians 1:15–20

For in Christ all the fullness of Deity lives in bodily form and you have been given fullness in Christ, who is the Head over every power and authority.

Colossians 2:9–10

Come along with me, let's find this man from Galilee. He is the Son of God, walk with Him and listen to Him until you've taken up your stand. Then soon, you'll want to talk to Him as He takes you by the hand.

May the words of my mouth
and the meditation of my heart
be pleasing to you,
O Lord, my Rock and my Redeemer. **Psalm 19:14**

Jesus Christ Rules

Although the world is so big and the people are so many, Jesus Christ still rules. Christ created the world, but the people He created didn't recognize Him (**John 1:10**). Even the people chosen by God to prepare the rest of the world for the Messiah rejected Him **John 1:11,** although the entire Old Testament pointed to His coming. **Commentary on John 1:10–12**

All who welcome Jesus Christ as Lord of their lives are reborn spiritually, receiving new life from God. Through faith in Christ, this new birth changes us from inside out—rearranging our attitudes, desires, and motives:

Jesus Christ is the suffering Savior of the Trinity.

Sent by the Father to those who love Him.

Believing is the Key.....Longing and waiting for the future.

"Therefore, if anyone is in Christ, he is a new creation; the old has gone, the new has come" **2 Corinthians 5:17**

When I was given this new life, many of my loved ones couldn't understand what had come over me. As a matter of fact, even I had to accept the changes according to my new commitment, or I wouldn't have understood what was happening, either. I only knew that I had asked Him to be my Lord and Savior, invited Him into my heart (life), and was ready and willing to see and welcome His presence in my life. He made His love so important to me. When I received the infilling of the Spirit, I knew without a doubt that He wanted me to share it with all those who would listen. This message I received was given in love for all to hear. Loved ones telling loved ones, friends telling friends. I wanted them to turn to Him instantly to see what a wonderful Savior and friend I had found. He is the most important person that anyone will ever meet. And so full of all the things we need, love, protection, and care, blessings and gifts forever!

How **does 2 Corinthians 5:17 fit** into your life? Do you want to be a new person? Is it important to you that your Creator is honored and held in reverence by everyone? Do you want the best for your loved ones? God already knows the answers to your needs. Most reflect the joy that He brings with His salvation as well as His power to call others.

In the Book of Jeremiah, He says: "I know the plans I have for you," declares the Lord. "Plans to prosper you and not harm you, plans to give you a hope and a future. Then you will call upon me and come and pray to me and I will listen to you. You will seek me and find me when you seek me with all your heart. I will be found by you," declares the Lord. **Jeremiah 29:11–14**

Have you searched for Him with all your heart, until you found Him? Do you feel like a new person? Is your life changing as a result of it? Are new friends coming into your life, and are they carrying their bibles?

Just reminiscing, as I remember the different places He took me and the new people who lavished a new language on me and found me prospering in the Word Of God.

Have you ever thought about being born dead when you found life in this world. What an awesome God we have to meet the challenge of our lives and create a new person that totally belongs to Him. One that now carries with him the hope of Eternity with God.

And what about the cost he paid for the words He spoke:

'I know the plans I have for you,' declares the Lord. 'Plans to prosper you and not to harm you, plans to give you a hope and a future.'

That is the greatest transaction that any human being could ever experience.

We are God's ambassadors…according to His words below**.**

Because we understand our fearful responsibility to the Lord, we work hard to persuade others.

God knows we are sincere, and I hope you know this, too. Are we commending ourselves to you again? No we are giving you a reason to be proud of us, so you can answer those who brag about having a spectacular ministry rather than having a sincere heart. If it seems we are crazy, it is to bring glory to God. And if we are in our right minds, it is for your benefit. Either way, Christ's love controls us. Since we believe that Christ died for all, we also believe that we have all died to our old life.

He died for everyone so that those who receive His new life will no longer live for themselves. Instead, they will live for Christ, who died and was raised for them.

So we have stopped evaluating others from a human point of view. At one time we thought of Christ merely from a human point of view. How differently we know Him now! This means that anyone who belongs to Christ has become a new person. The old life is gone; a new life has begun! And all of this is a gift from God, who brought us back to Himself through Christ. And God has given us this task of reconciling people to Him. For God was in Christ, reconciling the world to Himself, no longer counting people's sins against them. And He gave us this wonderful message of reconciliation. So we are Christ's ambassadors; God is making His appeal through us. We speak for Christ when we plead, 'Come back to God!' For God made Christ, who never sinned, to be the offering for our sin, so that we could be made right with God through Christ.

2 Corinthians 5:11-21

Chapter Six

How have we been crucified?

With Jesus in you.....you will live in and be like Jesus...!

Recapping the Trinity in chapter five. He alone is our God. He is our Father. He is our Savior. And He speaks to us in a voice so loving and tender. He sent Jesus His only Son to die for our sins; (He wants to become your personal God.) Jesus gave me His Holy Spirit. He is the only one who can remember my sins no more. Did He forget? Yes, He just doesn't remember them because Christ is light and life and sin is darkness and death, which is the opposite of life. When I invited Him into my heart it became His heart; and He gave me a new one, shinning with Christ. I came from the dark side of the mountain to the light side in the twinkling of His eye. The mystery: No one can ever find my old heart. When He replaced it (took it away), I died to Him.

Check: 2 Corinthians 5:17
He is our one and only God.
Convicted And Committed: We are Leading.

Legally God looks at us as if we had died with Christ While His Word is Helping us lead Others to Help Themselves.

There are two important questions that can open our minds to salvation. Ask yourself these questions. First: If you were to die today, are you sure that you would go to heaven. In a hypothetical setting the second question is: If you stood before Christ today and he ask you: (Place your name here as you listen to these words from Jesus, 'Why should I let you into my heaven?' What would you say? It won't happen that way, But what if it did? Again, may I suggest something for you to think about as you think of your response?

All churches and religions have one thing in common; they cannot save you! Salvation is a gift that you can only get through following Jesus. It comes in a personal relationship with Him...

Please commit to understanding these last three verses About Jesus; who He really is, and that He came from heaven just to get you and call you His very own.

See John 17:3 and John 3:3)

You must be born again.

2 Corinthians 5:17….. Paying Attention to Scripture

Therefore, I will always remind you about these things—even though you already know them and are standing firm in the truth you have been taught.

And it is *only* right that I should keep on reminding you as long as I live.

2 Peter 1:12-13

God's Plan to Help

Have you ever cleared your throat to get someone's attention? Maybe you waved your hand in front of their eyes? Honked your horn? Or maybe nothing you could do awakened their interest in you. God used a near-death situation to take my eyes off the world and get me to focus them on Him, or to use the words of our Lord, "Where your treasure is, there your heart will be also." Because we live in the world we think that our minds and hearts should always be focused on the things that we can think about, sense, or feel—the things that will support our bodies and the things that seem the most satisfying to our hearts and lives.

But I remember the first commandment or His words in **Jeremiah 29:11–14?** If remembering the words are important, committing our lives to them is really the necessary part. That is where we tend to lose our focus with Him if we remain uncommitted. Commitment and priority—or His will before mine—is the key to a relationship with Him.

The light comes on when we see Him for who He really is, a God who loved us so much that He sent Jesus to die in our place, for our sins. He really is a God who can say, "I know the plans that I have for you. Plans to prosper you, and not to harm you, plans to give you a hope and a future." Our future with Him includes all eternity. He holds all of our hopes in His hands as well as the love and well-being of our families.

How can we be perfect? **(1)** In character: In this life we cannot be flawless, but we can aspire to be as much like Christ as possible. **(2)** In Holiness: Like the Pharisees, we are to separate ourselves from the world's sinful values. But unlike the Pharisees, we are to be devoted to God's desires rather than our own and carry his love and mercy to the world. **(3)** In Maturity: We can't achieve Christ-like character and Holy living all at once, but we can grow toward maturity and wholeness. Just as we expect different behavior from a baby, a child, a teenager, and an adult, so God expects different behavior from us, depending on our stage of spiritual development **(4)** In Love: We can seek to love others as completely as God loves us. We can be perfect if our behavior is appropriate for our maturity level….Perfect, yet with much room to grow. Our tendency to sin must never deter us from striving to be more like Christ. Christ calls all of his disciples to excel, to rise above mediocrity, and to mature in every area, becoming more and more like him. Those who strive to become perfect will one day be perfect, even as Christ is perfect. **Commentary on Matthew 5:48 W/insights from (1 John 3:2-3)**

His Grace

I know there is a Savior who watches over all;

He is so dependable, He's near when 'ere we call.

His children learn to follow by the promise in His name.

Trusting in the Bible, His Word He will not stain.

His Word maintains a record for the oath by which He stands,

It shows us how He bound Himself with the power in His hands.

A power, oh so merciful, to display His awesome love,

Grounded by an oath secure in His promise from above.

There is a hope for all to claim; it is written in His Word,

Embodied by the truth where His oath finds us secured.

He called this oath unchangeable because He cannot lie.

In the promise of His Word, where believers never die.

Poem by Bob Bowman

Rescued By Jesus

With His Power And Grace given through the Holy Spirit.

When God created man, He created him to have fellowship with Him, His

loving maker in a beautiful place called heaven.

God didn't want man to feel he must love God, or be compelled to live with him, so He gave man a will of his own, but always demanded respect and obedience. In other words in human language we can understand, "If you don't appreciate this wonderful garden of mine, you may go and cultivate one of your own." Man chose to follow his own desires and disregard his Fathers words of wisdom and obedience.

In heaven there is in that place a tree of life. Eternal with God, and it yielded its own fruit of eternal blessings that would allow man's sinful presence to be with God, and never to die. God will not permit sin in His heaven. He is Holy.

In other words, disobedience or disrespect for God would always be in God's presence and his Kingdom would always be filled with sinners sin. and So man was put out of the Garden of Eden and, let's say, support himself instead of being taken care of by his Father in His real home, where man's attempt's are still being made to return in his own strength and wisdom.

God's Wisdom

The message of the cross is foolishness to those who are headed for

destruction! But we who are being saved know it is the very

saving power of God. **1 Corinthians 1:18**

Chapter Seven

Life in the Spirit

Looking back sternly at chapter six. Please Learn! How to be crucified with Christ. Pg. 72 How we are nothing without God in Christ. Pg. 118 Be an approved worker pg. 78 Live as citizens of heaven Pg. 78. Paul's work in the church. Are you heaven bound? 120-121 Winning the prize P.122-123 Who do you belong to? Summed up carefully in Chapter six. The bridge illustration on Pg. 125 shows bible verses that explain where we stand in Christ. Be There! Study and join the chorus of believers in Psalm 84 esp. 84:10 Has God placed any unbelievers on your heart today?

How Have We Been Crucified

With Christ ?

Legally God looks at us as if we had died with Christ. Because our sins died with Him, we are no longer strangers **Colossians 2:13-15** if we receive Him. Relationally, we have become one with Christ, and His experiences are ours. Our Christian lives began when, in unity with Him, we died to our old life. See **Romans 6:5-11** In our daily life we must regularly crucify sinful desires that keep us from following Christ. This, too, is a kind of dying with Him.. **Luke 9:23-25** And yet the focus of Christianity is not dying, but living. Because we have been crucified with Christ, we have also been raised with Him. **Romans 6:5** Legally, we have been reconciled with God **2 Corinthians 5:19** and are free to grow into Christ's likeness **Romans 8:29.** And in our daily life we have Christ's resurrection Power as we continue to fight sin. **Ephesians 1:19- 20** We are no longer alone but Christ lives in us…..He is our power for living and our hope for the future. **Colossians 1:27**

With His undeserved favor there are two important questions that can open our minds to salvation. Please ask yourself these questions.

First: If you were to die today, are you sure that you would go to heaven?

Your answer; Be honest! In a hypothetical setting the second question is: If you stood before Christ today and He asked you: Jesus speaking : 'Why should I let you into my heaven?' What would you say? It won't happen that way, but what if it did?

Place your name and response here: If your answers are no, please, let loose of your pride and talk to your minister. If he doesn't know how to answer you, change churches. He is wasting both of your times.

What is god saying as you listen to these words from Jesus. Given by the Holy Spirit in **John 17:3** and **John 3:3**

All Churches and religions have one thing in common; they cannot save you. *You must be Born again. Transformed into the likeness of Christ.* **Check out John 3:3**

*Look once again in **2 Corinthians 5:17** to understand the statement above.*

We were His enemies, yet called and justified. **Romans 5:8 and 1 John 4.**

Discerning False Prophets Dear friends, do not believe everyone who claims to speak by the Spirit. You must test them to see if the spirit they have comes from God. For there are many false prophets in the world. This is how we know if they have the Spirit of God: If a person claiming to be a prophet acknowledges that Jesus Christ came in a real body, that person has the Spirit of God. But if someone claims to be a prophet and does not acknowledge the truth about Jesus, that person is not from God. Such a person has the spirit of the Antichrist, which you heard is coming into the world and indeed is already here.

But you belong to God, my dear children. You have already won a victory over those people, because the Spirit who lives in you is greater than the spirit who lives in the world. Those people belong to this world, so they speak from the world's viewpoint, and the world listens to them. But we belong to God, and those who know God listen to us. If they do not belong to God, they do not listen to us. That is how we know if someone has the Spirit of truth or the spirit of deception.

Will your life Be different After you commit your life to Christ? Re-read 2 Corinthians 5:17

Life In The Spirit

"If you die in Christ, you will reign with Him….to die is to live….."

Has your faith taken you to the point of death for Christ. Better still, are you in the phase of your life with Jesus that has claimed you for Him? So, you have been crucified with Christ, and your sins have been nailed to the cross? Or haven't you yet died with him? That of course is a faith building statement, but one that demands a careful and complete study. But, how can you study it unless someone challenges you with that very important need to consider for your relationship with Jesus. The challenge that all of us have is to be able to reign with Him in everlasting life, as the thought expresses itself further in **2 Timothy 2:1-26.**

An Approved Worker

Work hard so you can present yourself to God and receive His approval. Be a good worker, one who does not need to be ashamed and who correctly explains the word of truth. Work Hard, He tells us in verse nineteen as follows in Galatians 2:19 "But God's truth stands firm like a foundation stone with this inscription:" 'The Lord knows those who are His,' and All who belong to the Lord must turn away from evil."

In order to remove deception we must make clear in our heart's the certain expression of faith that explains within us this question: "Have I committed my life to Jesus? Have I asked Him to live and reign in my heart? Am I truly depending on Him for the total forgiveness of my sins. Is He my Lord, and my God? YES ! He is the one I serve, and I look for no other God.

John the Baptist, while being held in prison for preaching Christ, and soon to be martyred, asked one of his own disciples this deep searching question in Luke 7:18 The disciples of John the Baptist told John about everything Jesus was doing. So John called for two of his disciples, and he sent them to the Lord to ask him, "Are you the Messiah we've been expecting, or should we keep looking for someone else?" They beheaded John for his faith in Jesus, yet how could John be still in doubt. I know the problem was cleared up in the heart of John before he was beheaded for the scriptures tell us how he was a forerunner of the Lord, sent expressly to clear the way of the Lord.

 So ends the quote that led us into this discussion. 'If you died with Christ, you will reign with Him! To die is to live!' Living your life with the certainty of a life in heaven. Committed and united with other true believers.

Live as Citizens of Heaven

Above all, you must live as citizens of heaven, conducting yourselves in a manner worthy of the Good News about Christ. Then, whether I come and see you again or only hear about you, I will know that you are standing together with one spirit and one purpose, fighting together for the faith, which is the Good News. Don't be intimidated in any way by your enemies. This will be a sign to them that they are going to be destroyed, but that you are going to be saved, even by God himself. For you have been given not only the privilege of trusting in Christ but also the privilege of suffering for him. We are in this struggle together. You have seen my struggle in the past, and you know that I am still in the midst of it. But you must continue to believe this truth and stand firmly in it. Don't drift away from the assurance you received when you heard the Good News. The Good News has been preached all over the world, and I, Paul, have been appointed as God's servant to proclaim it. **Philippians 1:27-30**

Paul's Work for the Church

I am glad when I suffer for you in my body, for I am participating in the sufferings of Christ that continue for His body, the church. God has given me the responsibility of serving His church by proclaiming his entire message to you. This message was kept secret for centuries and generations past, but now it has been revealed to God's people. For God wanted them to know that the riches and glory of Christ are for you Gentiles, too. And this is the secret: Christ lives in you. This gives you assurance of sharing his glory.

So we tell others about Christ, warning everyone and teaching everyone with all the wisdom God has given us. We want to present them to God, perfect in their relationship to Christ. That's why I work and struggle so hard, depending on Christ's mighty power that works within me. **Colossians1:23-29**

Paul (and bob) gives up his rights. "Even though I am a free man with no master, I have become a slave to all people to bring many to Christ." **1Corinthians 9:19**

Don't you realize that in a race everyone runs, but only one person gets the prize? So run to win! All athletes are disciplined in their training. They do it to win a prize that will fade away, but we do it for an eternal prize. So I run with purpose in every step. I am not just shadowboxing. I discipline my body like an athlete, training it to do what it should. Otherwise, I fear that after preaching to others I myself might be disqualified.

1**Corinthians 9:24-27**

Jesus said, 'The thief comes only to steal and kill and destroy; I have come that they may have life, and have it to the fullest.' **John 10:10**

As we look at the bridge illustration on page 142, we see that the left side show verses where man's sin are holding him back from crossing the bridge because of the declaration of sin. That man stands without forgiveness. He is unable to cross over to the other side where God has revealed his forgiveness through the promises made to man through His word. When man discovers God's mercy and forgiveness, he joyfully accepts Christ into his life and becomes a new man able to cross into God's presence.

Isaiah 59

Warnings against Sin

1. Listen! The Lord's arm is not too weak to save you,
    nor is His ear too deaf to hear you call.

2. It's your sins that have cut you off from God.
    Because of your sins, He has turned away
    and will not listen anymore.

Rejoice in the Lord always. I will say it again: Rejoice! Let your gentleness be evident to all. The Lord is near. Do not be anxious about anything, but in everything, by prayer and petition, with thanksgiving, present your requests to God. And the peace of God, which transcends all understanding, will guard your hearts and your minds in Christ Jesus.

Finally, brothers, whatever is true, whatever is noble, whatever is right, whatever is pure, whatever is lovely, whatever is admirable—if anything is excellent or praiseworthy—think about such things. Whatever you have learned or received or heard from me, or seen in me—put it into practice. And the God of peace will be with you. **Philippians 4:6-9**

Philippians 4:8 And now, dear brothers and sisters, one final thing. Fix your thoughts on what is true, and honorable, and right, and pure, and lovely, and admirable. Think about things that are excellent and worthy of praise. Keep putting into practice all you learned and received from me—everything you heard from me and saw me doing. Then the God of peace will be with you.

Chapter Eight

Fulfilling God's Great Commission

What Happened To The Good News on the sidewalks of America?

When the shepherds heard about the birth of Christ, they left their flocks, drawn by angels to Bethlehem, and then they returned glorifying God. From there the Good News spread around the world. Yet we, in our generation, fail to share the Good News of Jesus as the faithful believers did when our Messiah was born. Why do we hesitate to share that blessing to an unbelieving world, or even our relatives? Are those Shepherds witnesses against us? Our involvement should be the same as theirs.

People need the Lord and He commands us to fulfill God's Great Commission.

The shepherds left their flocks, drawn by angels to Bethlehem, and then they returned glorifying God.

From there the good news spread around the world and through the centuries. Why do we often fail to fulfill the Great Commission to spread the good news?

The Great Commission

Then Jesus came to them and said, "All authority in heaven and on earth has been given to me. Therefore go and make disciples of all nations, baptizing them in the name of the Father and of the Son and of the Holy Spirit, and teaching them to obey everything I have commanded you. And surely I will be with you always, to the very end of the age." **Matthew 28:18–20**

A person who is unemployed must answer three questions each week for unemployment benefits:

1. Are you ready to work?

2. Are you willing to work?

3. Are you able to work?

The shepherds left their flocks to see the new born savior. From that day on through the centuries people have left their position in life to serve Jesus.

Have you given up your life in this world (be transformed) for a spiritual life in Christ, and are you ready, willing, and able to follow (submit) to Jesus Christ, and willing to come under His authority and will for your life…

Bible Study

Become hungry for His word. Eager to do His will. Love people into His kingdom through His words. All accomplished with Jesus living in the life of a person.

If you have never had the perfect dream, here it is, and it is perfect, real, and it is free.

The Apostle Paul's Charges to Timothy

You have been taught the Holy Scriptures from childhood, and they have given you the wisdom to receive the salvation that comes by trusting in Christ Jesus. All Scripture is inspired by God and is useful to teach us what is true and to make us realize what is wrong in our lives. It straightens us out and teaches us to do what is right. Now the Holy Spirit tells us clearly that in the last times some will turn away from what we believe; they will follow lying spirits and teachings that come from demons. These teachers are hypocrites and liars. They pretend to be religious, but their consciences are dead. **1 Timothy 4:1–2**

If you have received the gift of salvation and know that it has saved you, are you obedient in sharing the Good News?

For God's Glory.

Here is the way I share it:

Finding Common Ground

Yet preaching the Good News is not something I can boast about. I am compelled by God to do it. How terrible for me if I didn't preach the Good News! If I were doing this on my own initiative, I would deserve payment. But I have no choice, for God has given me this sacred trust. What then is my pay? It is the opportunity to preach the Good News without charging anyone. That's why I never demand my rights when I preach the Good News. One of my favorite things to do. Finding common ground for everyone of His elect. This square is part of **1 Corinthians 9:16-27,** but it is relative to my demeanor.

Even though I am a free man with no master, I have become a slave to all people to bring many to Christ. When I was with the Jews, I lived like a Jew to bring the Jews to Christ. When I was with those who follow the Jewish law, I too lived under that law. Even though I am not subject to the law, I did this so I could bring to Christ those who are under the law. When I am with the Gentiles who do not follow the Jewish law, I too live apart from that law so I can bring them to Christ. But I do not ignore the law of God; I obey the law of Christ. When I am with those who are weak, I share their weakness, for I want to bring the weak to Christ. Yes, I try to find common ground with everyone, doing everything I can to save some. I do everything to spread the Good News and share in its blessings.

Don't you realize that in a race everyone runs, but only one person gets the prize? So run to win! All athletes are disciplined in their training. They do it to win a prize that will fade away, but we do it for an eternal prize. So I run with purpose in every step. I am not just shadowboxing. I discipline my body like an athlete, training it to do what it should. Otherwise, I fear that after preaching to others I myself might be disqualified. **1 Corinthians 9:16-27**

Is God equipping you to share His Good News? Do you feel His urgency? Do you act as if you are in a race?

Be strong and of good courage as you share some of your personal thoughts and let your prayers be heard.

Correct, Rebuke, and Encourage

They will say it is wrong to be married and wrong to eat certain foods. But God created those foods to be eaten with thanksgiving by people who know and believe the truth. Since everything God created is good, we should not reject any of it. We may receive it gladly, with thankful hearts. **1 Timothy 4:3-4**

I correct and discipline everyone I love. So be diligent and turn from your indifference. "Look! I stand at the door and knock. **Revelations 3:19**

If you hear my voice and open the door, I will come in, and we will share a meal together as friends. **Revelations 3:20**

Words Of Joy And Comfort

Before He instilled in me the gift of Joy and salvation I was blind to Him as well as His words and His will. I had no knowledge of the possibility 0f Him living with His Spirit inside me… Living in my heart. I knew of no one who needed a personal relationship with Him, aside from the clergy, not knowing if they themselves were saved. As a matter of fact I was under the impression that only Hitler kind of people would go the wrong way. I thought person's became pastor's because they had a strong intellect and chose the ministry because they felt a need for people to know more about God, so they could live a better life. Also, that they wanted dearly to protect society, and to give people a hope to live with. Possibly that is why many people today live for themselves, not knowing about a wonderful and merciful God who is always reaching out for them. It is not His Will that any person should perish !

Please read these scriptures below, then think about your answer to the question…..

Why Do people hesitate to share the love of Jesus? Haven't they experienced it yet?

Matthew 4:4-11 Matthew 4:19-26 Jesus always calls those who will follow Him.

Matthew 3:8-9 1 Peter 2:2-3 God planned you and has a plan for you. He wants you to be clean through the blood of Jesus.

Deuteronomy 3:8-20 If you follow Jesus you will live and be blessed.

2 Peter 1:12-13 Prophesy always comes from God but many times He reminds of His presence and our commands from Him. **2 Timothy 1:12-13** Follow the pattern of God's word. You can be sure if you trust in the Spirit's work.

Aspiration

My Jesus, I Love Thee
Gordon

William R. Featherston, 1846-1873   Adoniram J. Gordon, 1836-1895

1. My Je – sus, I love Thee, I know Thou art mine - For thee all the Fol – lies of sin I re – sign; My gra – cious Redeem – er, my Sav – ior art Thou: If ev – er I loved Thee, My Je – sus, 'tis now."

2. I love Thee be - cause Thou hast first lov–ed me And pur–chased my Par – don on Cal-va – ry's tree; I love Thee for wear – ring the Thorns on Thy brow: If ev - I loved Thee, my Je – sus, 'tis now.

3. I'll love Thee in Life, I will love Thee in death, and praise as long as Thou lend – est me breath; And say when the death – dew lies cold on my brow, "If ev – er I loved Thee, my Je – sus, 'tis now,"

4. In man – sions of glo - ry and end – less de – light, I'll ev – er a – dore Thee in heav –en so bright; I'll sing with the glit – ter – ing crown on my brow, "If ev – er I loved Thee, my Je – sus 'tis now."

Growing In Christ

The Two Questions, in Love, That Changed My Life

1. If you would die today, are you sure that you would go to Heaven?

2. In a hypothetical setting: If you stood before Christ today and He asked you, 'Why should I let you into my heaven'? What would you say? It won't happen that way, but what if it die?

Let's suppose that all you can think of are words that you were led to believe in and through confirmation or baptism, but you never really had a personal relationship with Jesus. To face the awful thought of not having been "Born Again." To trust Jesus Blood, knowing that it was shed for you, as well as all true believers.

In other you have never been taught that everyone must be confronted with "Jesus" either now, or after it is too late to be saved.

This book is being written so that all who read it will never hear these words recorded in Matthew seven twenty three.
But will be living with Jesus either here or in heaven.

But I will reply, 'I never knew you. Get away from me, you who break God's laws.' Then all will realize the importance of The Good News. **Matthew 7:23**

G R A C E God's Riches At Christ Expense. Knowing that the requirement's of the law were met in the Blood of Christ, and the true Christians debt was paid in full.

Isn't the love of Jesus something wonderful....to praise His name forever.

All churches and religions have one thing in common. None of them can save you. Salvation is a gift that only Jesus can give you in a personal relationship with him. **(see John 17:3 and John 3:3)** You must be born again....Of water (baptism) and the Blood of Jesus.

Can Baptism Save You ?

It is possible to go to Heaven without having been baptized, but don't go out into the world thinking you are going to Heaven because you have been baptized.

 Baptism is merely proclaiming God's glory for letting you know of His love, mercy, and forgiveness; for His salvation; and for letting us enjoy His care and protection while we live in this distant land until He comes again.

Having been born again before you were baptized, or in a spiritual condition of proclaiming the good news to the world you live in, and knowing and accepting His grace-filled promises of salvation preludes all conditions of righteousness.

Are you relying on some external experience i.e. baptism, confirmation…church membership, good works, etc. to get into heaven?

Could you list here in a few lines what exactly is your hope of spending forever back home with Jesus your redeemer and maker?

Jesus said: "I correct and discipline everyone I love. So be diligent and turn from your indifference."

Revelation 3:19-20 (New Living Translation)

"Look! I stand at the door and knock. If you hear my voice and open the door, I will come in, and we will share a meal together as friends. **Revelations 3:19-20**

Keep listening to His voice, given to you by the Holy Spirit.

"Holy Spirit Please Come"

Is having the assurance of Heaven something new to you? Did you know that finding the right path is the prerequisite of being heaven-bound ? What if highway 61 takes you to Heaven, but you are traveling on highway 16. "There is a way that seems right to a man, but in the end it leads to death." That is Gods word to us in **Proverbs 14:12.**

All of us must travel the same road that goes to Jesus. Remember, we will all stand before the judgment seat of God for the scriptures say, "As surely as I live, says the Lord, 'every knee will bend to me, and every tongue will confess and give praise to God. **Romans 14:10b & 11**

Do you study the scriptures? Is it your intentions to grow into the likeness of Christ? Finally, do you understand what you are reading as you read the bible? The eunuch, honestly confessed that he didn't until Philip explained it to him as recorded in **Acts 8:30-35.** Philip ran over and heard the man reading from the prophet Isaiah. Philip asked, "Do you understand what you are reading?" The man replied, "How can I, unless someone instructs me?" And he urged Philip to come up into the carriage and sit with him. The passage of Scripture he had been reading was this:

"He was led like a sheep to the slaughter. And as a lamb is silent before the shearers, He opened not His mouth. Who can speak of his descendants? For his life was taken from the earth." The eunuch asked Philip, "Tell me, was the prophet talking about himself or someone else?" So beginning with this same Scripture, Philip told him the Good News about Jesus.

Jesus asked the people of his time that question while he looked into their hearts and found their real condition in **Luke 10:23.**

"You search the Scriptures because you think they give you eternal life. But the Scriptures point to me! Yet you refuse to come to me to receive this life.

John 5:39-40

I found out that coming to Jesus without giving Him your life is useless…He wants you as you are when He chooses you this day, so He can make you who He wants you to be…' His disciple' test…God has Churches throughout the world that are life giving…leading people to Christ…

Does the church you're attending challenge you to receive Christ, if not, is it time to move on.

The Five Spiritual Laws:

These five statements will help you understand why we all so desperately need Jesus and his Sacrifice For Us. Look up each reference scripture and write your response

Ephesians 2:8-9 Not earned or deserved**… Romans 6:23**

Man is a sinner **Romans 3:23**… cannot save himself.**…Exodus 64: 6-7**

God is loving.…..Jeremiah 31:3

But He Is just as well: Therefore He must punish sin. Romans 6:23

Christ: …..Who He is: Infinite God Man Isaiah 9:6…Colossians 2:9-10;

⁸Each of the four living creatures had six wings and was covered with eyes all around, even under his wings. Day and night they never stop saying: "Holy, holy, holy is the Lord God Almighty, who was, and is, and is to come." Revelation 4:8

What He Did: He paid for our sins and purchased a place in Heaven, which he offers as a gift to all who 'Receive' Him. Fill in the blank before **Ephesians 2:8-9**

Your thoughts:

What is Faith ?…. **2 Corinthians 5:17** We must Receive Christ With A Trusting Faith… Not with a mere intellectual assent, but with visible signs. No Guessing or hesitation (Like The Judge Bringing Down The Gavel…..Decision time!

Jesus Last Three Words

Sins Debt: Paid In Full

As Jesus hung on the cross agonizing in pain, He declared, **"It is Finished." (John 19:30)** Man can do nothing else but trust in Jesus' Word's. Until this time, a complicated system of sacrifices had atoned for sins. Sin separates people from God, and only through the sacrifice of an animal, a substitute, could people be forgiven and become clean before God. But people sin continuously, so frequent sacrifices were required. Jesus, however, became the final and ultimate sacrifice for sin. The word "finished" is the same as "paid in full." Jesus came to finish God's work of salvation **(John 4:34 and 17:4)** to pay the penalty for our sins. With his death, the complex sacrificial system ended, because Jesus took all sin upon himself. Now we can approach God because of what Jesus did for us. Those who believe in Jesus' death and resurrection can live eternally with God and escape the penalty that comes from sin.

Commentary on John 19:30

Prayerfully reflect on the work of Christ on your behalf….He would have died for you if you were the only person that ever walked the face of the earth. **That is how He feels about the penalty of sin. Lost in hell…**Consider His words below. The Lord isn't really being slow about his promise, as some people think. No, He is being patient for your sake. He does not want anyone to be destroyed, but wants everyone to repent. **But the day of the Lord will come as unexpectedly as a thief**. Then the heavens will pass away with a terrible noise, and the very elements themselves will disappear in fire, and the earth and everything on it will be found to deserve judgment. Since everything around us is going to be destroyed like this what Holy and Godly lives we should live, looking forward to the day of God and hurrying it along. **2 Peter 3:9-10**

Chapter Nine

A Warning to the Shepherds

The thief's purpose is to steal and kill and destroy. My purpose is to give them a rich and satisfying life. **John 10:10**

A Warning To The Shepherds To Encourage And Support Our life in the Spirit. God's laws are meant to make us stronger and help us to keep the covenant that we have made with our Lord.

Psalm 119:92 tells us: ***If your instructions hadn't sustained me with joy, I would have died in my misery.***

Then in **Psalm 119:9-11** our Lord tells us how a young man can keep his life pure. "By living with all of our hearts dedicated to His Word." This keeps us from straying away from his commands. Our Pastors' lead us into the fields where we too can be shepherds as well. Jesus tells us the harvest is ready and waiting, but few are the laborers.

God Loves His sheep so much, that He warns all shepherds (Pastors, leaders, evangelists or whoever translates His mercy short of His real love for all men) to proclaim both their freedom from sin, and the cost that He was willing to pay for that freedom, that they may both love and obey Him.

Then in that passion serve Him with the real joy of who He really is. Nothing short of "My Father who Art In Heaven, Hallowed Be Thy Name, Thy Kingdom Come, Thy Will Be Done, on Earth As It Is In Heaven."

With this dedication as one fully committed to who our Lord really is in all His glory, with the gratitude and thanksgiving as recorded through His Word to Ezekiel, we are directed to open up His words as given by the Spirit for all to understand.

The word of the Lord came to me: "Son of man, prophesy against the Shepherds of Israel; prophesy and say to them: 'This is what the Sovereign Lord says: Woe to the shepherds of Israel who only take care of themselves! Should not shepherds take care of the flock? You eat the curds, clothe yourselves with wool and slaughter the choice animals, but you do not take care of the flock. You have not strengthened the weak or healed the sick or bound up the injured. You have not brought back the strays or searched for the lost. You have ruled them harshly and brutally. So they were scattered because there was no Shepherd, and when they were scattered they became food for all the wild animals. My sheep wandered over all the mountains and on every hill. They were scattered over all the earth, and no one searched or looked for them. 'Therefore, you shepherds, hear the word of the Lord: As surely as I live, declares the Sovereign Lord, because my flock lacks a shepherd and so has been plundered and has become food for all the wild animals, and because my shepherds did not search for my flock but cared for themselves rather than my flock, therefore O shepherds, hear the Word of the Lord: This is what the Sovereign Lord says: I am against the shepherds and will hold them accountable for my flock. I will remove them from tending the flock so that the shepherds can no longer feed themselves. I will rescue my flock from their mouths, and it will no longer be food for them. 'For this is what the Sovereign Lord says: I myself will search for my sheep and look after them.'

Ezekiel 34:1-11

Christians, aren't we reminded of our Pastor as well as all the committed men who have taken on the role of "Faithful Servants" who deliver unto us the very words of God, who carefully inserted the challenge to each one of us for "Following Jesus, knowing and trusting in his blood in a way of being crucified with him." Not ashamed to challenge us with these words…

Entering the Kingdom of God Doesn't happen when you die ! If you want to enter, It is now, before you die. Jesus died to make that possible for everyone. One of the benefits of submitting to God, by receiving Jesus, is that we become citizens of His Kingdom now… today…and it is forever.

Have you made that commitment ?

Christians should experience a bit of the Kingdom of Heaven here on earth.

Meditate on these scriptures and write down your thoughts. Think them through.

Revelations 3:19-20

Matthew 11:19 What does wisdom prove?

Acts 13:38-43?

Reaching for His Righteousness…..In The Light Of The Son

Hope for Restoration….. "In that day," says the Lord, "I will be the God of all the families of Israel, and they will be my people. This is what the Lord says: "Those who survive the coming destruction will find blessings even in the barren land, for I will give rest to the people of Israel."

Long ago the Lord said to Israel: "I have loved you, my people, with an everlasting love. With unfailing love I have drawn you to myself. **Jeremiah 31:1-3**

The God of Our Fathers.

The Father and the Son sent the Holy Spirit to fill our lives with love and to enable us to live by His power **John 3:16; Acts 1:8.** With all this loving care, how can we do less than serve Him completely? Read especially **Romans 5:5-10.**

We were weak and helpless because we could do nothing on our own to save ourselves. Someone had to come and rescue us. Not only did Christ come at a good time in history; He came at exactly the right time, according to God's own schedule. God controls all history, and He controlled the timing, methods, and results of Jesus' death.

"When we were utterly helpless, Christ came at just the right time and died for us sinners" **Romans 5:6.** These are amazing words. God sent Jesus Christ to die for us. Not because we were good enough, but because He loved us. Whenever you feel uncertain about God's love for you, remember that He loved you before you turned to Him. If God loved you when you were a rebel, He can surely strengthen you now that you love Him in return. The love that caused Jesus to die and rise victoriously from the grave, is the same love that sends the Holy Spirit to live in us and guide us every day. **See Romans 5:8.**

A Call to Love and to Obedience

"You must love the Lord your God and obey all his requirements, decrees, regulations, and commands.

Keep in mind that I am not talking now to your children, who have never experienced the discipline of the Lord your God or seen his greatness and his strong hand and powerful arm. **Deuteronomy 11:1-2**

Carefully read what God requires of those who love Him in Deuteronomy 10:10-22. What does He promise in return? Consider verses 14 through 17

If you reject Him and His Salvation He Tells us plainly, "As God's partners we beg you not to accept this marvelous gift of God's kindness and then ignore it.

For God says, At just the right time, I heard you.
On the day of salvation, I helped you. **2 Corinthians 6:1-2**

Indeed, the 'right time' is now. Today is the day of salvation. For this reason God sends them a powerful delusion so that they will believe the lie and so that all will be condemned who have not believed the truth but have delighted in wickedness.

2 Thessalonians 2:11

Would you commit your life to Jesus today? Repent and ask Him to save you, showing Him you are ready to follow Him in thought word and deed. To become involved in His word through obedience to it. Isn't that what He just ask of you?

"If You Die In Christ, You Will Reign With Him, To Die With Him In This Life Is To Live With Him In Heaven….."

God's Redeeming Power

One of the most awesome facts of the Bible causes great joy to my spirit when, by faith, I understand that the same power that saved me is the same power that raised Jesus from the dead. And God placed that power within me to use everyday of my life….even as I fail him so many times….Yet He receives my sorrowing repentance with the gladness of a loving Father. Our praises go to the Lord God almighty, for His mercy, love and forgiveness!

Speaking of the right time being now.

Soon a Samaritan woman came to draw water, and Jesus said to her, "Please give me a drink." He was alone at the time because His disciples had gone into the village to buy some food. The woman was surprised, for Jews refuse to have anything to do with Samaritans. She said to Jesus, "You are a Jew, and I am a Samaritan woman. Why are you asking me for a drink?" Jesus replied, "If you only knew the gift God has for you and who I am, you would ask me, and I would give you living water." "But sir, you don't have a rope or a bucket," she said, "and this is a very deep well. Where would you get this living water? And besides, are you greater than our ancestor Jacob who gave us this well? How can you offer better water than he and his sons and his cattle enjoyed?" Jesus replied, "People soon become thirsty again after drinking this water. But the water I give them takes away thirst altogether. It becomes a perpetual spring within them, giving them eternal life." "Please, sir," the woman said, "give me some of that water! Then I'll never be thirsty again, and I won't have to come here to haul water." "Go and get your husband," Jesus told her. *"I don't have a husband,"* the woman replied. Jesus said, "You're right! You don't have a husband–for you have had five husbands, and you aren't even married to the man you're living with now." "Sir," the woman said, "you must be a prophet. So tell me, why is it that you Jews insist that Jerusalem is the only place of worship, while we Samaritans claim it is here at Mount Gerizim, where our ancestors worshiped?" Nothing like changing the subject!

Jesus replied, "Believe me, the time is coming when it will no longer matter whether you worship the Father here or in Jerusalem. You Samaritans know so little about the one you worship, while we Jews know all about him, for salvation comes through the Jews. But the time is coming and is already here when true worshipers will worship the Father in spirit and in truth. **John 4:24**

The Father is looking for anyone who will worship Him that way. For God is Spirit, so those who worship Him must worship in Spirit and in Truth." The woman said, "I know the Messiah will come–the one who is called Christ. When He comes, He will explain everything to us." Then Jesus told her, "I am the Messiah!" Just then his disciples arrived. They were astonished to find him talking to a woman, but none of them asked Him why He was doing it or what they had been discussing. The woman left her water jar beside the well and went back to the village and told everyone, "Come and meet a man who told me everything I ever did! Can this be the Messiah?" So the people came streaming from the village to see Him. Meanwhile, the disciples were urging Jesus to eat. "No," he said, "I have food you don't know about." "Who brought it to Him?" the disciple asked each other.

Then Jesus explained: "My nourishment comes from doing the will of God, who sent me, and from finishing His work. Do you think the work of harvesting will not begin until the summer ends four months from now? Look around you! Vast fields are ripening all around us and are ready now for the harvest. The harvesters are paid good wages, and the fruit they harvest is people brought to eternal life. What joy awaits both the planter and the harvester alike! You know the saying, 'One person plants and someone else harvests.' And it's true. I sent you to harvest where you didn't plant; others had already done the work, and you will gather the harvest."

John 4:7-38

Did The Woman find nourishment in Christ that was completely different from any nourishment she had previously had?

Read **1 Corinthians 2:9-16**…What Is God Promising Those Who By Faith Believe, asking Jesus into their hearts? (Be sure to look up and read) 'God's Deep Secrets' refer to God's unfathomable nature and His wonderful plan—Jesus' death and resurrection—and the promise of salvation, revealed only to those who believe that what God say's is true. Those who believe in Christ's death and resurrection and put their faith in Him will know all they need to know to be saved. This knowledge, however, can't be grasped by even the wisest people who don't know unless they accept God's message. All who reject God's message are foolish, no matter how wise the world thinks they are. **1 Corinthians 2:10**

Here lies the beauty of reading and knowing the Bible. Trusting in the Holy Spirit we prophesy as the Lord calls us to speak for Him. Jesus assures us that He is The Way, The Truth, And The Life, and promises us to be by our side with Him and actually speaks for us as we proclaim His great glory.

Paul spoke with authority because the Holy Spirit gave it to him. Paul was not merely giving his own personal views or his personal impression of what God had said. Under the inspiration of the Holy Spirit, he wrote the very thoughts and words of God.

Commentary on 1 Corinthians 2:13

The Spiritual, Natural, and Carnal Men

Does a difference in nourishment explain the difference in these three men? Why and How?

What does the Word of God have to say about the three different kinds of men: the spiritual man, the natural man, and the carnal man?......Only the Spiritual man can bring the Good News to your soul. Others may try but they are without the Holy Spirit as well as God's Power and their words actually turn into lies, because they aren't speaking from God's heart, but their own. Normally their words are based on their own emotions which God cannot bless, because they lack the Truth and the Power of God. A better way of saying all of this is summed up in just Five words in John 3:3....You Must Be Born Again.

The Spiritual Man

We have not received the spirit of the world but the Spirit who is from God, that we may understand what God has freely given us. This is what we speak, not in words taught us in human wisdom but in words taught by the Spirit, expressing spiritual truths in spiritual words. **1 Corinthians 2:12–13**

The Natural Man

The man without the Spirit does not accept the things that come from the Spirit of God, for they are foolishness to him, and he cannot understand them, because they are spiritually discerned. **1 Corinthians 2:14**

The Carnal Man

Dear brothers and sisters, when I was with you I couldn't talk to you as I would to mature Christians. I had to talk as though as you belonged to this world, or as though you were infants in the Christian life. **1 Corinthians 3:1**

Only The Spiritual man can represent God. The natural and the carnal man remain uncommitted, possibly because of their unbelief or because they may not want total responsibility....unfaithful servants that may not totally believe God's Word. They don't understand the truth's that only God can speak through his Spirit, so they remain disconnected and for the most part don't even understand that they lead sad lives for themselves and for their families. The hard fact is they aligned themselves with an unbelieving seminary that taught them these untruths. They could have just been in the ministry as an easy way to make a living.

Characteristics of a Natural man

No one can know what the Lord is thinking **Romans 11:34,** but through the guidance of the Holy Spirit, believers have insight in some of God's plans, thoughts, and actions. They, in fact, have "the mind of Christ." Through the Holy Spirit, we can begin to know God's thoughts, talk with Him, and expect His answers to our prayers. Are you spending enough time with Christ to have His very mind in you? An intimate relationship with Christ comes only from spending time consistently in His presence and in His Word. We who have the Spirit understand these things, but others can't understand us at all. How could they? For, "Who can know what the Lord is thinking? Who can give him counsel?" But we can understand these things, for we have the mind of Christ. **Commentary on 1 Corinthians 2:16**

"I assure you, unless you are Born again, you can never see the Kingdom of God."

John 3:3

Characteristics of a Carnal Man

Brothers, I could not address you as spiritual but as worldly—mere infants in Christ. I gave you milk, not solid food, for you were not ready yet for it. Indeed you are still not ready. You are still worldly. **1 Corinthian 3:1-3**

- **Lives in the comfort zone**

- **Can't stand "the heat"**

- **Bears fruit**—ugly fruit• Has mixed loyalties• Is a hearer, not a doer• Yet he is not hopeless. God's design is for us to be radical Christian's, passionately in love with Him. He is a jealous God and will not settle for second place.

A Chosen Life Study.

Christianity, Obedience, and the Narrow Road

Are you amazed and incredulous? Do you not believe it? Then go ahead and be blind if you must. You are stupid, but not from wine! You stagger, but not from beer! For the LORD has poured out on you a spirit of deep sleep. He has closed the eyes of your prophets and visionaries. All these future events are a sealed book to them. When you give it to those who can read, they will say, "We can't read it because it is sealed." When you give it to those who cannot read, they will say, "Sorry, we don't know how to read." And so the Lord says, "These people say they are mine. They honor me with their lips, but their hearts are far away. And their worship of me amounts to nothing more than human laws learned by rote. Because of this, I will do wonders among these hypocrites. I will show that human wisdom is foolish and even the most brilliant people lack understanding."

Wake Up Destruction is certain for those who try to hide their plans from the Lord, who try to keep him in the dark concerning what they do! The Lord can't see us,' you say to yourselves. "He doesn't know what is going on!" How stupid can you be? He is the Potter, and he is certainly greater than you. You are only the jars he makes! Should the thing that was created say to the one who made it, "He didn't make us?" Does a jar ever say, 'The potter who made me is stupid?' **Isaiah 29:9–16**

This explains who the unrepentant sinner is that has allowed his conscience to be shipwrecked.

Antidote: Let God's Spirit draw you back to Him through Jesus by the 'sorrow' of repentance. With a willingness of the heart while responding to a faith which is based on John 3:3.

Chapter 10

When I Was Just A Boy
His Command Are Very Good

They Enable Us To Really Love Our Neighbor

"I command you–be strong and courageous!"

For the Lord your God is with you wherever you go.

Dear Lord, I know that you remember me when I was just a boy,

When I was very little and lived without your joy.

I didn't know for many years, when you died upon the cross,

That all my sins were paid for, it was you that bore the cost.

I thought that I could just be good and honor You that way,

But then I learned about your Word and all the things You say

I couldn't believe the pain You bore for such a one as I,

Until I looked into your word and heard Your mournful cry.

It was just as though I stood there, consenting to your death;

I heard You say, "My God, My God," while taking your last breath.

"Why has thou forsaken me?" your heart begin to cry,

And then your pain was ended as darkness filled the sky.

But I had lived so many years not knowing of your plan

That sent you to the cross of shame for such a sinful man.

Lord, I am very sorry now, you mean so much to me,

And I am very thankful that you died to set me free.

Still bless me as I walk anew to share your precious Word

That others also may rejoice in the gospel they have heard.

Please guard their souls, enlighten them…. With your Spirit so secure

That in their time of struggle………… your victory will endure.

Poem by Bob Bowman

The Lord taught us these Commands in **Joshua 1:6-9** Be strong and courageous, for you will lead my people to possess all the land I swore to give their ancestors. 'Be strong and very courageous. Obey all the laws Moses gave you. Do not turn away from them, and you will be successful in everything you do.

Study this Book of the Law continually. Meditate on it day and night so you may be sure to obey all that is written in it. Only then will you succeed. **Joshua 1:9**

Make your effort deep and committed even after you are born of the water and the blood; That you may fight of the schemes of Satan. Statement found in John chapter three verse three.

Jesus replied, I tell you the truth, Bob, unless you are born again, you cannot see the Kingdom of God.   **John 3:3**

When I was just a boy ! I hadn't the faintest idea of what God expected of me, even with a desire to please Him, in my subconscious mind, without intent; yet without searching for Him. I didn't know His Word was His meeting place, and had no desire to devour it like food from the table. I thought it was terrible the way those cruel men killed Jesus, but I couldn't find a fault within myself.

Yet, I played a game in my mind that whenever I committed a sin I would pound a nail in a board. Then, when I done something good I would pull the nail out. (Of course I would always begin with the worst sin, and may have not remembered many more. *I remember concentrating on being good until I felt the guilt had been removed.*

Finally it came to pass that all the nails were gone, but such a frustrating thing filled my heart. All the marks that the nails made were still there. (imagination) I thought to myself. He knows what I have done in my life, but I passed it off with, 'Oh well, it's too late for me to change the score'. I grew up trying to be someone God would care for, and miraculously, He did. But should of He, I reasoned. Still, He let me love Him and it seemed like such a wonderful love affair. I thought He cared a lot for me, yet I was unsaved and without the knowledge of salvation. My testimony is in the beginning of this book, so I won't go into that again, except to tell you that the relationship that He let me have, developed into a love for the people in my life. When he saved me that love for others was sort of magnified, and in trying to understand it I realized it wasn't my love at all. It was His love trying to love people through me. When I got it all together I was able to share the Good News with a deep and committed passion. My thinking about it made it simple. I am blessed if He wants to use me, although I didn't understand how a person as sinful as myself, could be chosen by God to walk close to Him. He has a marvelous character and I am the least of all men to be gifted with that fellowship, while being completely undeserving.

I live in a condition of faith that seems so natural; handed to me by Grace without my knowledge of how I could be chosen for such an important job in this world. Free to give, and Free to share. I really can't understand how anyone can live without faith.

Evangelical Insights

My greatest prayer is that I will always be given the wisdom and understanding to do His will. *It will always be a mystery to me while I live here, separated from Him by the flesh, how I became involved with such a wonderful and loving God. This I have found true through intimate contacts.*

There were a group of words that I spoke to Him in the hospital that marked the beginning of my blessed journey. They seemed very simple but very true as I recall them at the time, and as I find myself embedded in them now. Simply put here they are: "God, today I died." My life is over, and my life doesn't belong to me any more, it is yours. All I ask was an opportunity to say goodbye to my wife, and family and you gave me a life in this world surrounded by a family with love for me; and life with a future. So, today my life belongs to you.

If you would like to know another one of his loving connections that night, be sure to memorize John 10:10, because He will tell you the same thing He told to me. It was one of his first spiritual magnets that He used with me.

The thief's purpose is to steal and kill and destroy. My purpose is to give them a rich and satisfying life. **John 10:10**

Another was 1 Peter 1:2-3….I would be cheating you if I didn't share this one with you. His words follow:

Like newborn babies, you must crave pure spiritual milk so that you will grow into a full experience of salvation. Cry out for this nourishment, now that you have had a taste of the Lord's kindness. **1 Peter 1:2-3**

This ends the story, and the reason for the poem, "When I was just a boy.**" But as this story ends, the excitement of another story quickly unfolds, and by the grace of God, I know and pray that it will continue till I see Jesus. The story is about fishing ! Before I begin, I need to tell you that I never went looking for bait, or enjoyed setting on river banks. I also must tell you that I had no desire to catch the biggest fish…..But,**

Jesus furnished the bait, which was His Word empowered by His Spirit, and it seems like He loves the little fish equally as well as the big ones. It is also noteworthy to mention that as the little fish feasted on His bait some turned into very big fish [people]; the kind with big hearts that attract other little [people].

If there seems to be something fishy about this story, go to the book of Revelations and check in at Chapter three verses 19 and 20.

There you'll find that before you get a pole to go fishing, you will need to get an invitation. The invitation reads like this:

I correct and discipline everyone I love. So be diligent and turn from your indifference. "Look! I stand at the door and knock.

If you hear my voice and open the door, I will come in, and we will share a meal together as friends. **Revelations 3:19-20**

For your listening ears you will see that after the meal you will find yourself feeling loved and setting at the feet of Jesus. If that doesn't happen go back to verse one and read the first eighteen verses. If that hasn't settled firmly in your heart then bless yourself with verses 21 and 22. If by this time you feel blessed, we have become brothers in the greatest event that has ever taken place in the heart of man.

Why is it insufficient to say "You belong to Christ, unless indeed you are called and scripturally formed?"

Read Isaiah 29:9-16 as well as Revelation 3:19-20 and find your explanation here.

Find Love In This Text Instead Of Lecture.

Compare it to Revelation 3:19-20

***This day I call heaven and earth as witnesses against you that I have set before you life and death, blessings and curses. Now choose life, so that you and your children may live and you may love the Lord your God, listen to His voice and hold fast to Him. For the Lord is your life, and He will give you many years in the land he swore to give to your fathers, Abraham, Isaac and Jacob.* Deuteronomy 30:19-20**

We find these words of comfort: Don't worry about anything; instead, pray about everything. Tell God what you need, and thank Him for all He has done. Then you will experience God's peace, which exceeds anything we can understand. His peace will guard your hearts and minds as you live in Christ Jesus.

And now, dear brothers and sisters, one final thing. Fix your thoughts on what is true, and honorable, and right, and pure, and lovely, and admirable. Think about things that are excellent and worthy of praise. Keep putting into practice all you learned and received from me—everything you heard from me and saw me doing. Then the God of peace will be with you. **Philippians 4:6-9**

Continuing on the way to: Knowing Jesus. Knowing Him better, with the confidence that He is surely by your side after you have received Him into your heart.

In your mind *and by your prayer* that you have invited him into your heart with a positive knowledge that you need Him there. For life and for salvation.

No one deserves that, but it is Free......For the asking.

At the time of the sacrifice, I stood up from where I had sat in mourning with my clothes torn. *I fell to my knees and lifted my hands to the Lord my God. I prayed, 'O my God, I am utterly ashamed; I blush to lift up my face to you. For my sins are piled higher than my head, and my guilt has reached to the heavens.* From the days of our ancestors until now, we have been steeped in sin. That is why we and our kings and our priests have been at the mercy of the pagan kings of the land. We have been killed, captured, robbed, and disgraced, just as we are today.

"But now we have been given a brief moment of grace, for the Lord our God has allowed a few of us to survive as a remnant. He has given us security in this holy place. Our God has brightened our eyes and granted us some relief from our slavery. For we were slaves, but in his unfailing love our God did not abandon us in our slavery. Instead, he caused the kings of Persia to treat us favorably. He revived us so we could rebuild the Temple of our God and repair its ruins. He has given us a protective wall in Judah and Jerusalem. "And now, O our God, what can we say after all of this? For once again we have abandoned your commands! Your servants the prophets warned us when they said, 'The land you are entering to possess is totally defiled by the detestable practices of the people living there. From one end to the other, the land is filled with corruption.

Ezra 9:5–11...made personal

I believe God gave us these words of Ezra for a very special reason. And so, I am especially pleased and thankful to make room for it in the book "A Chosen Life Study." I have ask myself these questions:

How many times in sorrow have I, Bob, fell to my knees? "O my God, I am utterly ashamed; I blush to lift up my face to you. For our sins are piled higher than our heads, and our guilt has reached to the heavens.

"But now we have been given a brief moment of grace, for the Lord our God has allowed a few of us to survive as a remnant. He has given us security in this holy place. Our God has brightened our eyes and granted us some relief from our slavery. Amen!

Fishers of Men.

God's desire is that we share our relationship with Him and draw others to Jesus.

Seek the Lord while He may be found; call on Him while he is near. Let the wicked forsake his way and the evil man his thoughts. Let him turn to the Lord, and He will have mercy on him, and to our God, for He will freely pardon. **Isaiah 55:6–7**

Have I not commanded you? Be strong and courageous. Do not be terrified; do not be discouraged, for the Lord your God will be with you wherever you go. **Joshua 1:9**

I thank Christ Jesus our Lord, who has given me strength, that He considered me faithful, appointing me to His service. Even though I was once a blasphemer and a persecutor and a violent man, I was shown mercy because I acted in ignorance and unbelief. The Grace of our

Lord was poured out on me abundantly, along with the faith and love that are in Christ Jesus. Here is a trustworthy saying that deserves full acceptance: Christ Jesus came into the world to save sinners—of whom I am the worst. But for that very reason I was shown mercy so that in me, the worst of sinners, Christ Jesus might display His unlimited patience as an example for those who would believe on Him and receive eternal life. Now to the King eternal, immortal, invisible, the only God, be honor and glory for ever and ever. Amen.

1 Timothy 1:12–17

I strain to reach the end of the race and receive the prize for which God, through Christ Jesus, is calling us up to heaven. I hope all of you who are mature Christians will agree on these things. If you disagree on some point, I believe God will make it plain to you. **Philippians 3:14–15**

Are You Willing to Be a Zacharias?

In Luke 19 Zacchaeus showed his willingness to have a relationship with Jesus. Jesus entered Jericho and was passing through. A man was there by the name of Zacchaeus; he was a chief tax collector and was wealthy. He wanted to see who Jesus was, but being a short man he could not, because of the crowd. So he ran ahead and climbed a sycamore-fig tree to see him, since Jesus was coming that way. When Jesus reached the spot, He looked up and said to him, "Zacchaeus, come down immediately. I must stay at your house today." So he came down at once and welcomed him gladly. (Is it any wonder people respond quickly to Jesus' voice?)

All the people saw this and began to mutter, "He has gone to be the guest of a 'sinner."

But Zacchaeus stood up and said to the Lord, "Look, Lord! Here and now I give half of my possessions to the poor, and if I have cheated anybody out of anything, I will pay back four times the amount." Jesus said to him, "Today salvation has come to this house, because this man, too, is a son of Abraham. For the Son of Man came to seek and to save what was lost." **Luke 19:1–10**

Then Jesus said to his disciples, "If anyone would come after me, he must deny himself and take up his cross and follow me. For whoever wants to save his life will lose it, but whoever loses his life for me will find it. What good will it be for a man if he gains the whole world, yet forfeits his soul? Or, what can a man give in exchange for his own soul? **Matthew 16:24–26**

What is the cost of choosing Christ? And following Him?

Look in **Matthew 10:37-39**

What is the cost of not following? Look at **Luke 12:4-5**

How do we follow Jesus? He left all of His tracks in the bible.

Each track has the words "Shed for you. " "Take time to be Holy."

Your vessel and your mode of travel.

Long ago the Lord said to Israel: "I have loved you, my people, with an everlasting love.

With unfailing love I have drawn you to myself. Jeremiah 31:3

My confirmation verse!…..Why is it that the light didn't come on for 28 years?…Surely, God is Long-suffering!

But, please don't be blinded by the world and it's sight's like I was.

Was God forced to save me because I was confirmed? In my own mind it took much more than that? It took the blood of Jesus, which I hadn't recognized, or turned to at the time. Was it His Spirit? Or was it my mind overpowering my heart that God was really calling me to "Receive His Son" out of His Godly mercy?

Just what is Habakkuk saying?

I have heard all about you, Lord.
I am filled with awe by your amazing works.
In this time of our deep need,
help us again as you did in years gone by.
And in your anger,
remember your mercy. I see God moving across the deserts from Edom,
the Holy One coming from Mount Paran.
His brilliant splendor fills the heavens,
and the earth is filled with his praise.
His coming is as brilliant as the sunrise.
Rays of light flash from his hands,
where his awesome power is hidden. **Habakkuk Chapter 3:2-5 ?**

Pestilence marches before him;

plague follows close behind.

Complete the test. What Rewards are there for making **2 Corinthians 13:5** your centerpiece?

Motivation for salvation is and must be a desire for loving and obeying the Lord. His (Father's) plan, His (Son's) purpose, His (Holy Spirit's) power—all were given for you! What an amazing gift!

His presence intervened without hesitation because God had a plan and a purpose for my life. It is a wonderful plan full of love and protection while we live in this dangerous and sinful world. His gift also has a wonderful retirement plan for you and your family. Think of it ! He died to make that come true. Simply because he loves us with an unexplainable love.

Attention!

How Easy Do We All Overlook This?

"No one can serve two masters. For you will hate one and love the other; you will be devoted to one and despise the other. You cannot serve both God and money."

The Pharisees, who dearly loved their money, heard all this and scoffed at Him. Then He said to them, "You like to appear righteous in public, but God knows your hearts. What this world honors is detestable in the sight of God. **Luke 16:13-15**

In Philippians 1:3-11, also Phil 2:1-3; 2 Thessalonians. 2:3-17

And 1 Thessalonians 4:1-10.

What happens when we love more and more? Who do we love?

I was changed into the likeness of Christ when I was 41, and given a character much different than when I was young. "I want to pour out my praise to Him forever, and bless His Holy name, and yet Satan still works on my sinful nature; My old life without Christ lasted too long. He (Satan) creates evil desires attempting to recapture my old life, even today, but Jesus "Our Lord" promises He will never leave me or forsake me. He gives each one of us the power to be victorious. The Roaring Lion is unable to harm us spiritually with Jesus within us, and defending us in the life we now have with Him.

This is the very reason that I use so much Scripture in A Chosen Life.

When I became a Christian, scripture became alive for me.

And made alive with God.....A New Creation !

Why be like the pagans who are deeply concerned about their life?

Your heavenly Father already knows all your needs, and He will give you all you need from day to day <u>if you live for Him and make the Kingdom of God your primary concern.</u>

Matthew 6:32-33

When we were born, we were born into a world where sin reigns. Most people don't understand that until Christ comes victoriously into their lives.....Not without a personal invitation, however, He allows us to have our own free will, He works in our lives until we finally realize that without him our lives are involved in a movement which leads us away from Him.

The heart is always lonesome if it isn't filled with Christ, being moved in the direction of His love. He created us to have fellowship with Him, and through that fellowship we learn what is right and what is not only wrong, but that which leads us away from Him and hinders our fellowship with Him.

To make the Kingdom of God your primary concern means to put Christ first in your life. Now **(when Christ enters your life)** <u>He</u> is the driver and we are the passengers of our earthly vessel. That requires the process of **being 'Born Again,'** or, giving Him his real position in our lives, Prophet, Priest, and King.....The director of all our lives, while living within us. Hence comes the verse where he tells us plainly. "

Don't you realize that your body is the temple of the Holy Spirit, who lives in you and was given to you by God? You do not belong to yourself, for God bought you with a high price. So you must honor God with your body." **1 Corinthians 6:19-20**

Read the following verses in your bible and tell what happens when other things compete for first place in our lives. What does it say about you when you try to serve multiple masters.

Seeking His Righteousness…as you read and observe: **James 4:4 and John 2:15**

 Luke 16:13-15 James 1:19-25 1 John 2:15-17

Now comes the application as we pray for God's will and His way.

When we put Christ First, we become a blessing to others.

Look in the areas of your bible below, as you find yourself…..In the light of His Son.

Philippians 1:3-11

Philippians 2:1-32

Thessalonians 2:13-17

James 4:4 You are not faithful to God. Don't you know that to be a friend of the world is to hate God? Anyone who chooses to be a friend of the world becomes an enemy of God.

1 John 2:15 Do not love the world or anything in it. If you love the world, love for the Father is not in you.

Drawing Close to God.

What is causing the quarrels and fights among you? Don't they come from the evil desires at war within you? You want what you don't have, so you scheme and kill to get it. You are jealous of what others have, but you can't get it, so you fight and wage war to take it away from them. Yet you don't have what you want because you don't ask God for it. And even when you ask, you don't get it because your motives are all wrong—you want only what will give you pleasure. You adulterers! Don't you realize that friendship with the world makes you an enemy of God? I say it again: If you want to be a friend of the world, you make yourself an enemy of God.

James 4:1-3

The Full Armor Of God

Ephesians 6:13-17 (New Living Translation)

[13] Therefore put on the full armor of God, so that when the day of evil comes, you may be able to stand your ground, and after you have done everything, to stand. [14] Stand firm then, with the belt of truth buckled around your waist, with the breastplate of righteousness in place, [15] and with your feet fitted with the readiness that comes from the gospel of peace. [16] In addition to all this, take up the shield

of faith, with which you can extinguish all the flaming arrows of the evil one. [17] *Take the helmet of salvation and the sword of the Spirit, which is the word of God.*

The Full Armor Of God

In Poetic Form

The full armor of God, are you using Him today?

To protect against the evil one and his darts along your way.

Some days I forget Him, and the devil sees me go;

he's always prowling 'bout me to strike a heavy blow.

But Jesus always rescues me, He picks me up each time;

Reminds me of His armor that I had left behind

It isn't hard to choose, for you He will adorn,

The devil cannot touch you then, he can see you've been reborn.

So gird your loins with truth, take the breastplate of righteousness,

Shod your feet with His Gospel, then go about and bless.

You have the shield of faith, be sure it goes along.

With the helmet of salvation, He has made you very strong.

With the sword of the Spirit, which is the Word of God,

The equipment of the Gospel, your feet have now been shod.

Your shield will keep you company, for that is our Dear Lord,

Don't go anywhere without Him, He's your helmet and your sword. **Poem By Bob Bowman**

Chapter 11

A Chosen Life Study
This Life in the Spirit
A call to Christ as a young man

While we are young, we are less appreciative regarding "The Things Of God." And as Life gets its hold on us, we are less concerned about the bible and the things that God has appointed for us to do. We are so easily deceived, between serving Him and serving the world. God wants us to live a sure and spiritual life, centered around the Father, His Son and the power of the Holy Spirit. His blessings and curses are recorded for us.

This day I call heaven and earth as witnesses against you, that I have set before you life and death with signs and curses. Now choose life, so that you and your children may live and love the Lord, listen to His voice and hold fast to Him. For the Lord is your life, and He will give you many years in the land he swore to give to your fathers, Abraham, Isaac and Jacob. Strength always comes from His Word. Everything we face in life, we can draw on God's Word for our strength, and comfort. **Deuteronomy 30:29-30**

1 Samuel 14:6 (New International Reader's Version)

1 Samuel 14:6 Jonathan spoke to the young man who was carrying his armor. He said, "Come on. Let's go over to the camp of those fellows who aren't circumcised. Perhaps the Lord will help us. If he does, it won't matter how many or how few of us there are. That won't keep the Lord from saving us."

Bible Study

We opened up His Word, His commandments to obey.

The study in Colossians, 2:7 points the way.

It tells us to be steadfast, to be grounded so secure,

In love that speaks of sacrifice, in unity so sure.

He gave us all the message that tells about One Way,

Showed us a life eternal, a Truth we must obey.

He brought us close together, our lives are not the same,

In Christ we're bound together, for now there is no stain.

His message is so clear, just listen to this word,

"Abide in Me and I in you, for eternity secured.

If anyone can hear my voice and opens up the door,

I will come in unto Him and fellowship evermore."

So come to Him who labor, who carry the load of sin,

He promises a new life to all who ask Him in.

For everyone who believeth and trust His Holy name,

Will have a life eternal, washed clean from every stain.

All this He has written on the tablets of our hearts,

Gave us a love for sharing, in a world that's torn apart.

This love says, "God has spoken" in these last days by His Son.

He came into a world of sin to die for everyone. **Poem by Bob Bowman**

Examine these Verses First before studying
Faith Roots and Depth.

Luke 16:13-15; James 4:4; and 1 John 2:15-16

Faith, Roots, Depth..... & ..... Likeness To Christ

Let your roots grow down into Him and draw up nourishment from Him, so you will grow in faith, strong and vigorous in the truth you were taught. Let your lives overflow with thanksgiving for all He has done. **Colossians 2:7**

Without wavering, let us hold tightly to the hope we say we have, for God can be trusted to keep his promise. **Hebrews 10:23**

He provides fellowship for all who have a longing for Him. To walk, and to serve with Him, drawing others to the fold…Hence.. **John 1:12-14** But to all who believed him and accepted him, he gave the right to become children of God. They are reborn—not with a physical birth resulting from human passion or plan, but a birth that comes from God. So the Word became human[and made his home among us.

Let us think of ways to motivate one another to acts of love and good works. And let us not neglect our meeting together, as some people do, but encourage one another, especially now that the day of his return is drawing near. **Hebrews 10:24-25**

The three boxes below are some powerful words from the Lord, and they changed a mediocre faith on my part to a stirring faith. Not only for myself, but for every human soul.

He provides amazing grace and spiritual growth. So now you Gentiles are no longer strangers and foreigners. You are citizens along with all of God's Holy people. You are members of God's family. We are his house, built on the foundation of the apostles and the prophets. And the cornerstone is Christ Jesus Himself. We who believe are carefully joined together, becoming a Holy temple for the Lord. Through him you Gentiles are also joined together as part of this dwelling where God lives by His Spirit. **Ephesians 2:19-22**

He teaches us to say, "Not our will but yours, O Lord." "Not all people who sound religious are really Godly. Important: What is religious and what is Godly?

Matthew 7:21-24 They may refer to me as 'Lord,' but they still won't enter the Kingdom of Heaven. The decisive issue is whether they obey my Father in heaven. On judgment day many will tell me, 'Lord, Lord, we prophesied in Your name and cast out demons in Your name and performed many miracles in Your name.' But I will reply, 'I never knew you. Go away; the things you did were unauthorized. Anyone who listens to my teaching and obeys me is wise, like a person who builds a house on solid rock.

Why were their teachings unauthorized? Good question!

The Holy Spirit must be manifested in the person's heart before He can be known to represent the 'Father.' The Father knows His own, and those who have Jesus living in their heart. Not simply a casual believer. Thus, You must be born again. **John 3:3-8**

God's Secret Wisdom

Below is an article in the bible on the redemption of man, by justification in Jesus Christ.

There is a wisdom, not included in this chapter, that all people who haven't received Christ follow. Together they agree with each other as to what the bible calls a 'Wisdom of the world.'

In doing so they separate themselves from Christians who interpret the bible fluently as words from God. He supplies them with the faith and direction He wants them to have, and with it leads them, 'like a shepherd leads his sheep.'

Glorify God with your life in Christ-- John 3:3

Made Alive with Christ:

Ephesians 2 Once you were dead because of your disobedience and your many sins. You used to live in sin, just like the rest of the world, obeying the devil—the commander of the powers in the unseen world. He is the spirit at work in the hearts of those who refuse to obey God. All of us used to live that way, following the passionate desires and inclinations of our sinful nature. By our very nature we were subject to God's anger, just like everyone else. But God is so rich in mercy, and he loved us so much, that even though we were dead because of our sins, he gave us life when he raised Christ from the dead. (It is only by God's grace that you have been saved!) For he raised us from the dead along with Christ and seated us with him in the heavenly realms because we are united with Christ Jesus. So God can point to us in all future ages as examples of the incredible wealth of his grace and kindness toward us, as shown in all he has done for us who are united with Christ Jesus.

God saved you by his grace when you believed. And you can't take credit for this; it is a gift from God. Salvation is not a reward for the good things we have done, so none of us can boast about it. For we are God's masterpiece. He has created us anew in Christ Jesus, so we can do the good things he planned for us long ago. Oneness and Peace in Christ.

Don't forget that you Gentiles used to be outsiders. You were called "uncircumcised heathens" by the Jews, who were proud of their circumcision, even though it affected only their bodies and not their hearts. In those days you were living apart from Christ. You were excluded from citizenship among the people of Israel, and you did not know the covenant promises God had made to them. You lived in this world without God and without hope. But now you have been united with Christ Jesus. Once you were far away from God, but now you have been brought near to him through the blood of Christ. For Christ himself has brought peace to us. He united Jews and Gentiles into one people when, in his own body on the cross, he broke down the wall of hostility that separated us. He did this by ending the system of law with its commandments and regulations. He made peace between Jews and Gentiles by creating in himself one new people from the two groups. Together as one body, Christ reconciled both groups to God by means of his death on the cross, and our hostility toward each other was put to death.

He brought this good news of peace to you Gentiles who were far away from him, and peace to the Jews who were near. Now all of us can come to the Father through the same Holy Spirit because of what Christ has done for us.

A Temple for the Lord.

So now you Gentiles are no longer strangers and foreigners. You are citizens along with all of God's holy people. You are members of God's family. Together, we are his house, built on the foundation of the apostles and the prophets. And the cornerstone is Christ Jesus himself. We are carefully joined together in him, becoming a holy temple for the Lord. Through him you Gentiles are also being made part of this dwelling where God lives by his Spirit.

Examine again 1 Peter 1:1-2 and 1 Peter 2:1-7

The Hope of Eternal Life

All praise to God, the Father of our Lord Jesus Christ. It is by his great mercy that we have been born again, because God raised Jesus Christ from the dead. Now we live with great expectation, and we have a priceless inheritance—an inheritance that is kept in heaven for you, pure and undefiled, beyond the reach of change and decay. And through your faith, God is protecting you by his power until you receive this salvation, which is ready to be revealed on the last day for all to see.

Now to Him who is able to establish you by my gospel and the proclamation of Jesus Christ, according to the revelation of the mystery hidden for long ages past, but now revealed and made known through the prophetic writings by the command of the Eternal God, so that all nations might believe and obey Him—to the only wise God be glory forever through Jesus Christ! Amen. **Romans 16:25–27**

So get rid of all evil behavior, Bob. Be done with all deceit, hypocrisy, jealousy, and all unkind speech. Like newborn babies, Bob, you must crave pure spiritual milk so that you will grow into a full experience of salvation. Cry out for this nourishment, Bob, now that you have had a taste of the Lord's kindness.

Living Stones for God's House.

You are coming to Christ, Bob, who is the living cornerstone of God's temple. He was rejected by people, but He was chosen by God for great honor. And you are living stones that God is building into his spiritual temple. What's more, you are his holy priests, Bob. Through the mediation of Jesus Christ, Bob, you offer spiritual sacrifices that please God.   **1 Peter 2:1-5**

A Call to Holy Living

So think clearly and exercise self-control. Look forward to the gracious salvation that will come to you when Jesus Christ is revealed to the world. **1 Peter 1:10-13**

Can anyone be saved if they don't honor Him in His Word?

So we must listen very carefully to the truth we have heard, or we may drift away from it. For the message God delivered through angels has always stood firm, and every violation of the law and every act of disobedience was punished. So what makes us think we can escape if we ignore this great salvation that was first announced by the Lord Jesus Himself and then delivered to us by those who heard Him speak? And God confirmed the message by giving signs and wonders and various miracles and gifts of the Holy Spirit whenever he chose. **Hebrews 2:1–4**

Let's talk about Justification

God's love is not something that can be explained in our minds. It isn't easily understood until everything comes together, by searching the depths of our soul to partially get the vision of who we really are. Woe is me! By nature an enemy of God.

But you may say wholeheartedly, "I don't want to be His enemy; no, I love God the Father of our Lord Jesus Christ." Still, by our very nature, it took the innocent shed-blood of Jesus to cleanse us permanently from hell, death and destruction.

Would you like to see the before and after He enters our hearts? (to be born again) It gives us a clear picture of who we are and where he wants us to go.

The thief's purpose is to steal and kill and destroy. My purpose is to give them a rich and satisfying life. **John 10:10**

John 10:10-17 I am the good shepherd. The good shepherd sacrifices his life for the sheep. A hired hand will run when he sees a wolf coming. He will abandon the sheep because they don't belong to him and he isn't their shepherd. And so the wolf scatters the flock. The hired hand runs away because he's working only for the money and doesn't really care about the sheep.

I am the good shepherd; I know my own sheep and they know me, just as my Father knows me and I know the father. So I sacrifice my life for the sheep. I have other sheep, too, that are not in this sheepfold. I must bring them also. They will listen to my voice, and there will be one flock with one shepherd.

The Father loves me and He sent Jesus into my life to exchange my old life, so that I might take His in exchange, and live for Him in Christ. Happy Easter, folks, the resurrection just took place. **End John 10:10-17**

Now let's talk about the Why Of Justification.

How does anyone become justified. Consider yourself when you were born. You grew up into a family who should have shown a lot of love for you. That's the way God planned it. If that occurred in your life, you are familiar with doing as you were told in a loving way; and also in a way that the other members of your family have established themselves in a behavioral mode. So you feel attached and are very happy inside.

When you go out among the people of world you expect the same conditions that prevailed in your loving family. But very soon you see the world taking you places you know are wrong, and you begin to notice the home atmosphere is gone.

Does it matter to you? **Really matter?** If it does, you may choose to live a Holy life. God sees your heart and comes to your rescue. He knows the course of your life because He created you for His purpose. But there is still a problem. **That is what God says in Isaiah 59.** We all have the same seed. Adam and Eve brought it to us and only God Almighty can change it. That is why He lovingly sent His Son. Full of Mercy He came to redeem us.....To make us His very own!

Explained it to us in Isaiah 59 as follows:

Isaiah 59

Warnings against Sin:

Listen! The Lord's arm is not too weak to save you,

nor is his ear too deaf to hear you call.

It's your sins that have cut you off from God.

Because of your sins, he has turned away

and will not listen anymore. **Isaiah 59:1-2**

My heart is bleeding 4 U to become justified. My experience is that all hearts must invite our Lord and Savior Jesus into their heart, of course in a passionate way, because of the great love and mercy He has shown for all people! If you were the only person in the world he would have came to earth and died for you. In full control of His being, He dismissed His Spirit in death for you Saying, It Is Finished in **John 19:30.**

But now you heed the words that tell us why we need to be justified. To be drawn near to God through Jesus. Jesus said, "I am the way, the truth, and the life. No one can come to the Father except through me. If you had really known me, you would know who my Father is. From now on, you do know him and have seen him. Have you met the Lord Jesus?

John 14:6-7

Philip said, "Lord, show us the Father, and we will be satisfied." Jesus replied, "Have I been with you all this time, Philip, and yet you still don't know who I am? Anyone who has seen me has seen the Father."

So, have you seen Him? Follow Him closely in His Word. His invitation is follow me! Listen for His voice…It is far different than any other. **Revelation 3:17-22**

You say 'I am rich. I have everything I want. I don't need a thing!' And you don't realize that you are wretched and miserable and poor and blind and naked. So I advise you to buy gold from me---gold that has been purified by fire. Then you will be rich. Also buy white garments from me so you will not be ashamed by your nakedness, and ointment for your eyes so you will be able to see. I correct and discipline everyone I love. So be diligent and turn (get justified) from your indifference. Continued on page 131,

"Look! I stand at the door and knock. If you hear my voice and open the door,

(of your heart) I will come in, and we will share a meal together as friends. **Those** who are victorious (overcome your humanness) will sit with me on my throne, just as I was victorious and sat with my Father on his throne. 'Anyone with ears to hear must listen to the Spirit and understand what he is saying to the churches' (His command carries responsibilities, just like the ones you followed in the loving family that you still love so much----your earthly family). **Now you have two families!** One on earth and one in heaven. God says you need to share His wonderful blessing with your first family, and friends. Will you do it now that you have been justified by believing and receiving His word into your <u>heart</u>? **Revelation 3:17-22**

Justified!

The miracle of faith, and the connection with God that enables Him to call ua justified is translated vigorously in God's Word. But does being justified make us different from the rest of the world? Does He love me more than people who haven't been justified? Yes, and no! I accepted His love in order to follow Him. Many turn Him down because of His commands to follow Him. He gave all of us a free will. Most people miss the gift that caused Him to send His only Son to the cross of shame to suffer, so those who love Him will accept His mercy and follow.

God hates sin! It disrupted our fellowship with Him. But He loves the sinner. He knew me and shared His mercy with me. Miraculously, I understood and received the only solution to my problem that He has to offer. His Son, Jesus Christ. The One and Only, who was given to all who would die to Him, sacrificing their life in this world to serve Him, and to be His own possession. When properly understood it allow His Blood to flow threw us in a way that allows His crucifixion to be one of our own. We also died in order for us to live for Him, and we live and have our being in Him. Now I sin, but I'm not a sinner. What's the difference you may ask? He instilled in me a hatred for sin, so I repent and ask him for strength not to do it again. If you really want to see a heart full of sorrow for His sins read Roman's chapter seven.

I can only speak for myself in this manner, but, because I have been justified I can now come into His presence to love him, to praise Him, and to thank Him for the way he changed me from inside out. I ask Him to forgive me each time I'm convicted of sin. The curtain was torn from top to bottom in the Holy place of His presence, so, I need not carry around the load of sin any longer. I can take the hurt of my sin to

 Him and ask for His forgiveness, as well as His help in avoiding the hurt of that sin happening again. Now I have a happy feeling inside and He calls it 'His Joy,' and after living with it for 35 years, I call it my joy.

Because of it, while always remembering the Blood that Christ that was shed for my sins, I have been delivered into the everlasting joy that He daily fills my life and heart with, and I continually praise Him for his special gift of total forgiveness and the blessed hope for the home He has prepared for me when I leave this world.

The very thought of seeing Him, knowing Him as my Lord and Savior goes far beyond the imagination, that I will walk with Him in the garment of salvation that He died to provide me with.

He calls me to love the dedicated servants in this life who are preaching Christ and Him Crucified to the point of walking up to them after a service, in the joy that I speak of, and give them a hug. I always ask myself the question: Does Jesus give hugs? Maybe that's what He means when He says' in his Word....Love your neighbor as yourself. I will 'wipe every tear from their eyes.'Justified by His grace.....What a wonderful feeling of Joy! Loving hearts goes far beyond hugs, it is much deeper, as Christians know. Yes, He is Risen Indeed! It is the language of real Love.

How do I escape from this body of sin, to be justified and called 'A child of God?' Fully qualified to call Him Father and allowed to speak to Him at will even more fluently than my own Dad ? List some reasons. I will get us started.

1. Jesus died and rose again for our justification. Think of your past and bring it up to the present with **2 Corinthians 5:17**

2.

3.

4.

5.

The articles in justification reveal the beauty that He glamorizes His children with. Create a love song with these words."You are mine, because I am yours."'for you have made me your child.'

Listen, Please Listen And Hear

I was dust and you made me a dwelling, to live and proclaim your word,

I was dead and you brought me to life, to speak and proclaim, your words I have heard.

I fell and you picked me up, was blind and you opened my eyes,

You gave me a breath and words to speak, my burden was light as I echoed your cries.

The world is sleeping beneath your wings, with many a doubtful heart,

Your love cries out in mercy, while their lives are straying, yes falling apart.

Refusing to grasp your calling each day, your pleadings are reaching deaf ears, 'The music is playing the gospel so clear,' 'wake up, oh wake up, sinner,' and know that His coming is near.
Poem By Bob Bowman

This righteousness from God comes through faith in Jesus Christ to all who believe. There is no difference, for all have sinned and fall short of the glory of God, and are justified freely by His grace through the redemption that came by Christ Jesus.

God presented Him as a sacrifice of atonement, through faith in His Blood.

Romans 3:22–25a

Paul uses this verb, 'justified,' twenty-two times, mostly through Galatians chapters 2 and 3 while it is translated 'declared righteous.' *The term describes what happens when someone believes in Christ as his or her Savior. From the negative view point, God declares the person to be not guilty……From the positive view point, He declares him to be righteous. He cancels the guilt of the person's sins and credits righteousness to him. Paul emphasizes two points in this regard:*

No one lives a perfectly good, Holy, righteous life. On the contrary, 'there is no one righteous' (Romans 3:10), and 'all have sinned and fall short of the glory of God' (verse 23). 'Therefore no one will be declared righteous in His (God's) sight, observing the law' (verse 20).

But even though all are sinners and not sons, God will declare everyone who puts his faith in Jesus not guilty but righteous (verse 26). This legal declaration is valid because Christ died to pay the penalty for our sins and lived a life of perfect righteousness that can be imputed to us. This is the central theme of Romans and is stated in the theme verse, 1:17, 'a righteousness from God.' Christ's righteousness is obedience to God's law, and His sacrificial death will be credited to believers as their own. Are we trying to pat ourselves on the back again? No, we are giving you a reason to be proud of us, so you can answer those who brag about having a spectacular ministry rather than having a sincere heart before God.

Romans 2:13 to 5:1

God made him who had no sin to be sin for us, so that in him we might become the righteousness of God. **2 Corinthians 5:21**

Paul uses the word 'credited' nine times in chapter 4 alone. Freely by His grace—the central thought in justification is that although man clearly and totally deserves to be declared guilty **(Romans 9–19)** because of His trust in Christ, God declares Him righteous. This is stated in several ways here. Paul affirms the humanity and divinity of the mystery of Our Faith. The secret of how we become Godly 'appeared in the flesh' Jesus was a man; Jesus is the basis of our being right with God. 'Was shown to be righteous by the Spirit' Jesus resurrection showed that the Holy Spirit's Power was in Him. **(Romans 8:11)** . 'Was seen by the Angels': and was taken Up Into Heaven.'…..Jesus is divine. We cannot please God on our own; We must depend on Christ. **1Timothy 3:14-16 com.**

Why The Scale That Balances Is Out Of Balance

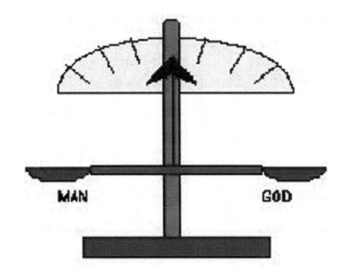

When the Unbalanced Scale Has the Proper Spiritual Focus

Man:

Sinner

Fallen

Doomed

Helpless

God:

Risen

Exalted

Merciful

Forgiving

Many people believe that the fatherhood of God means the brotherhood of men. Scripture plainly teaches that because God is holy, man must individually conform to His plan. "Be perfect, therefore, as your heavenly Father is perfect" (Matthew 5:48). There is no God who will save man collectively, according to the holy Scriptures. Ritualism or religion that is passed on from one generation to the next cannot save unless Jesus Christ and the power of His resurrection is the hope and center. All ministries that exalt the Lord God will confidently preach Christ and Him crucified.

We have a society today that seems to demand self-esteem. In reality, self-esteem is satisfied by trusting Jesus Christ completely for one's eternal security and the gift of sharing that with others. What purpose is there for man to live apart from Christ? Can a branch produce grapes without the vine? "What good is it for man to gain the whole world and yet lose or forfeit his very self?" **(Luke 9:25)** God is our Father, but that doesn't transform men into spiritual brothers. Christ came to do that.

(see 2 Corinthians 5:17).

Listen to Jeremiah: "To whom can I speak and give warning? Who will listen to me? Their ears are closed so they cannot hear. The word of the Lord is offensive to them; They find no pleasure in it. But I am full of the wrath of the Lord, and I cannot hold it in." **Jeremiah 6:10-11**

People suffer from spiritual decay and disease and are not aware of it **(see Jeremiah 6:7).** 'They dress the wounds of my people as though they were not serious. 'Peace, peace,' they say when there is no peace. Are they ashamed of their loathsome conduct? No, they have no shame at all; they do not even know how to blush. So they will fall among the fallen; they will be brought down when I punish them, says the Lord'. **Jesus saves the vilest sinner. Jeremiah 6:14-15**

Though our sin keeps us from God, His Mercy draws us near.

Reaching For Righteousness…..In The Light Of he Son

Isaiah 64:6 All of our works are like filthy rags. We can never be good enough.

Isaiah 53:6 Jesus suffered so we could be by believing in His atoning blood.

Romans 3:23 We are dead in our sins.

Romans 6:23 But alive in Christ. Indeed, if we have intentionally received Him.

Revelation 3:19-20 To receive and obey.

Psalm 143:2 ² Don't take me to court and judge me,
 because in your eyes no living person does what is right.

Which of the above verses describes our need for God; Which ones describe God's Mercy.

1. "Freely" as a gift—for nothing

2. "By His grace"

3. "Through the redemption that came through Christ Jesus"

4. "Through faith" (verse 25)

"Redemption"—a word taken from the slave market. The basic idea is that of obtaining release by payment of a ransom. Paul uses this word to refer to release from guilt with its liability for judgment and to deliverance from slavery to sin because Christ in His death paid the ransom for us. Open your heart for Jesus to enter. **Commentary from Romans 3:24**

Apart From Christ, Or In Christ.

Do you recognize his authority, or, the joy of His Presence ?

Read again Revelation 3:19 through 22

Have you discovered the power of the Holy Spirit; and do you depend on him in the daily issues of your life ? Of Course we all need help with this.

Have you been declared not guilty before the throne of God. Is Jesus there defending you, or will you face His rod?

My dear children, I write this to you so that you will not sin.

But if anyone does sin, we have one who speaks to the Father in our defense—Jesus Christ, the Righteous One. He is the atoning sacrifice for our sins, and not only ours but also for the sins of the whole world. We know that we have come to know Him if we obey his commands.
1 John 2:1–3

I know very well how foolish the message of the cross sounds to those who are on the road to destruction. But we who are being saved recognize His message as the very power of God. As the Scripture says, 'I will destroy human wisdom and discard their most brilliant ideas.

1 Corinthians 1:18

This Life in the Spirit

You came near when I called you, and you said, "Do not fear." O Lord, you took my case; You redeemed my life. **Lamentations 3:57–58**

For it is by grace you have been saved, through faith—and this is not from yourselves, it is a gift of God—not by works, so that no one can boast.

Ephesians 2:8–9

Entering the Kingdom of God Doesn't happen when you die ! If you want to enter, It is Now before you die !

One of the benefits of submitting to God, by receiving Jesus is that we become citizens of His Kingdom now…Today…And it is forever

Have you made that commitment?

As God's partners, we beg you not to accept this marvelous gift of God's kindness and then ignore it. For God says,

"At just the right time, I heard you.
On the day of salvation, I helped you.

"Indeed, the "right time" is now. Today is the day of salvation.

2 Corinthians 6:1-2

Christians experience a bit of the Kingdom of Heaven here on earth. Meditate on these scriptures listed here on page 137 and write down your thoughts. What does the verses imply? What do you want to do about them. Where can you receive help?

Reaching for His Righteousness…..With The Light Of The Son

Deuteronomy 6:1-15

Matthew 7:13-14

1 John 2:15-18

Deuteronomy 8:3

James 2:9-21

Your unfailing love is better than life itself; how I praise you!

I will praise you as long as I live, lifting up my hands to you in prayer.
You satisfy me more than the richest feast.
I will praise you with songs of joy.

I lie awake thinking of you, meditating on you through the night. Because you are my helper I sing for joy in the shadow of your wings. Cling to you; your strong right hand holds me securely. **Psalm 63:3-8**

Those who live in the shelter of the Most High will find rest in the shadow of the Almighty. This I declare about the Lord: He alone is my refuge, my place of safety; he is my God, and I trust him. For he will rescue you from every trap and protect you from deadly disease.

He will cover you with his feathers. He will shelter you with his wings.

His faithful promises are your armor and protection. **Psalm 91:1-4**

Come Along With Me….Let's Talk To Jesus, From Galilee

Lord Jesus, I believe! You know every page my life and nothing about me is unknown to you. Could you help me Lord? Allow me to draw even closer to you. I believe your word is true, and by staying close to your word, I can walk with you. Let your word dwell richly in my heart and life, while abiding in your power & wisdom, I will grow more and more like you. I love to share your word with my friends and loved ones, **so that by reading, receiving and obeying, they too will become your child.**

The winds are blowing and the rains are coming, but tuck these words in your heart and Treasure them. Never let them go!

How can a young person stay pure?

**By obeying your word I have tried hard to find you—
don't let me wander from your commands.
I have hidden your word in my heart,
that I might not sin against you…. Psalm 119:9-11**

Here are the results of such a person:

Jesus shouted to the crowds, 'If you trust me, you are trusting not only me, but also God who sent me. For when you see me, you are seeing the one who sent me. I have come as a light to shine in this dark world, so that all who put their trust in me will no longer remain in the dark.' **John 12:44-46**

Be strong and of Good Courage

'When an evil spirit leaves a person, it goes into the desert, seeking rest but finding none. Then it says, 'I will return to the person I came from.' So it returns and finds its former home empty, swept, and in order. Then the spirit finds seven other spirits more evil than itself, and they all enter the person and live there. And so that person is worse off than before.' That will be the experience of this evil generation.' **Mathew 12:43-45**

Jesus is the Way to the Father, so "Don't let your hearts be troubled. Trust in God, and trust also in me. There is more than enough room in my Father's home. If this were not so, would I have told you that I am going to prepare a place for you? When everything is ready, I will come and get you, so that you will always be with me where I am." **John 14:1-3**

With Jesus Living in our hearts, Satan cannot overpower us.

Jesus defeated Satan at the cross, and all power is in God almighty's hand.

The Almighty Himself will be your treasure. He will be your precious silver! "Then you will take delight in the Almighty and look up to God. You will pray to him, and He will hear you and you will fulfill your vows to Him. You will succeed in whatever you choose to do, and light will shine on the road ahead of you. If people are in trouble and you say, 'Help them 'God will save them. Even sinners will be rescued; they will be rescued because your hands are pure." **Job 22:25-30**

Special Note: When you personally receive **Jesus 'The Christ,'** as Lord, your hands will become pure, and He will teach you repentance.

Use **Matthew 7:13-14** to cross reference with **Matthew 12:43-45.**

And never forget this: **Romans 8:34-37** states.... Who then will condemn us? No one—for Christ Jesus died for us and was raised to life for us, and He is sitting in the place of honor at God's right hand, pleading for us. Can anything ever separate us from Christ's love? Does it mean He no longer loves us if we have trouble or calamity, or are persecuted, or hungry, or destitute, or in danger, or threatened with death? (As the Scriptures say, "For your sake we are killed every day; we are being slaughtered like sheep.") No, despite all these things, overwhelming victory is ours through Christ, who loved us. Romans 8:34-37.

Proverbs 18:10.....The name of the Lord is a strong fortress; the godly run to him and are safe.

2 Timothy 2 As a Good Soldier of Christ Jesus This is a trustworthy saying:

If we die with him,
we will also live with him.
If we endure hardship,
we will reign with him.
If we deny him,
he will deny us.
If we are unfaithful,
he remains faithful, (Jesus never denies the repentant sinner)
for he cannot deny who he is.

My heart begs you and I to examine line one…If we die with Him.

Peace To You With His Joy

May the peace of God be with you; His love surrounds me now,

He walks with me continuously, wipes troubles from my brow.

And all His love is waiting; if you open up your heart,

He fills your life with all His joy, tears all your fears apart.

It's such a peaceful kingdom as He lives in you each day,

You offer all the pieces, in His hands you are the clay.

But you must be a part of it, give Him your precious soul,

You will become His temple, on earth you have a goal.

His love from you will bubble, and excitement soon will start,

His overflowing presence will be living in your heart.

He will change your daily living, give rhythm to your stride,

Awaken you to sinfulness, His grace with you will ride.

He gives you new directions, His love you will address,

You want to take His message of hope to all the rest.

For it is not the Father's will you're lost eternally,

That's why He sent His Son to us to die in misery.

But Jesus didn't die in vain, salvation is at hand.

Two thousand years of love exist, for you to take a stand.

Call Him to your daily life, the choice is yours alone,

In Him you'll find true happiness, For you His light has shown.

Poem by Bob Bowman

Chapter twelve

A Chosen Life Study
His Peace

"I am leaving you with a gift—peace of mind and heart. And the peace I give is a gift the world cannot give. So don't be troubled or afraid. Remember what I told you: I am going away, but I will come back to you again. If you really loved me, you would be happy that I am going to the Father, who is greater than I am. I have told you these things before they happen so that when they do happen, you will believe.

John 14:27-29

"If you love me, obey my commandments.

And I will ask the Father, and he will give you another Advocate, who will never leave you. He is the Holy Spirit, who leads into all truth. The world cannot receive him, because it isn't looking for him and doesn't recognize him. But you know Him, because He lives with you now and later will be in you. No, I will not abandon you as orphans—I will come to you. Soon the world will no longer see me, but you will see me. Since I live, you also will live. When I am raised to life again, you will know that I am in my Father, and you are in me, and I am in you. Those who accept my commandments and obey them are the ones who love me. And because they love me, my Father will love them. And I will love them and reveal myself to each of them." **John:14:15-21**

Jesus replied, "All who love me will do what I say. My Father will love them, and we will come and make our home with each of them. Anyone who doesn't love me will not obey me. And remember, my words are not my own. What I am telling you is from the Father who sent me. I am telling you these things now while I am still with you. But when the Father sends the

123

Advocate as my representative—that is, the Holy Spirit—He will teach you everything and will remind you of everything I have told you." **John 14:23-26**

Of course you would like me to recap the words above with a statement of my own regarding our peace.

Can you tell me the difference between His Peace and the peace we call our own? Before we were saved I rarely thought of our children's salvation. As a matter of fact we had no idea it took place in this life…we thought it was after this life…and everyone would be judged on their good behavior. So, what do we do now that we are a part of their destiny? They are ours to care for in a spiritual way, carefully teaching them the way of salvation. And that being done as surely as seeing that they have nourishment for their bodies.

Why spend your money on food that does not give you strength? Why pay for food that does you no good? Listen to me, and you will eat what is good. You will enjoy the finest food…. **Isaiah 55:2**

As I live, says the Lord God, you shall not have occasion any more to use this proverb in Israel. Behold, all souls are Mine; as the soul of the father, so also the soul of the son is Mine; the soul that sins, it shall die. **Ezekiel 18:3-4**

We can leave all of our concerns with God, and through prayer he will graciously take care of them. But what about our human wisdom, and our attempting to help God ? To be a part of the work in his kingdom.

The Bible tells us to train up a child in the way he should go and when he is older he will not depart from it. What is the order that belongs to us for training this child. I earnestly believe that belonging to a Church that has a Gospel speaking minister. Speaking Christ, and Him crucified, is the first step. Have an open relationship with your Pastor and the second concern in caring for the child's needs as well as your own. Make raising your children in Jesus the number one priority in your family life. When we do that, everyone benefits and it almost guarantees that we will satisfy the heart of Jesus. We will even recognize the thief on the cross. Jesus will most certainly take care of that and won't it be wonderful to be his neighbor. I doubt that he will even be able to tell us the bad part of his life, because his sins have been washed away.

Children and Parents:

Children, obey your parents because you belong to the Lord Jesus, for this is the right thing to do.

"Honor your father and mother." This is the first commandment with a promise: If you honor your father and mother, "things will go well for you, and you will have a long life on the earth. "Fathers, do not provoke your children to anger by the way you treat them. **Ephesians 6:1-4**

Coming Together In The Unity Of Faith

And it is impossible to please God without faith. Anyone who wants to come to Him must believe that God exists and that He rewards those who sincerely seek Him. **Hebrews 11:6**

Everyone should be able to see plainly why the bible is so complete in telling us about Jesus. Everything He say's has meaning for our relationship with Him, and for others. **For example read John 14:23-26.** These are explicit commands that need our attention. **We need the Holy Spirit** to understand and fulfill. We can't have the Holy Spirit without Jesus living in our hearts.

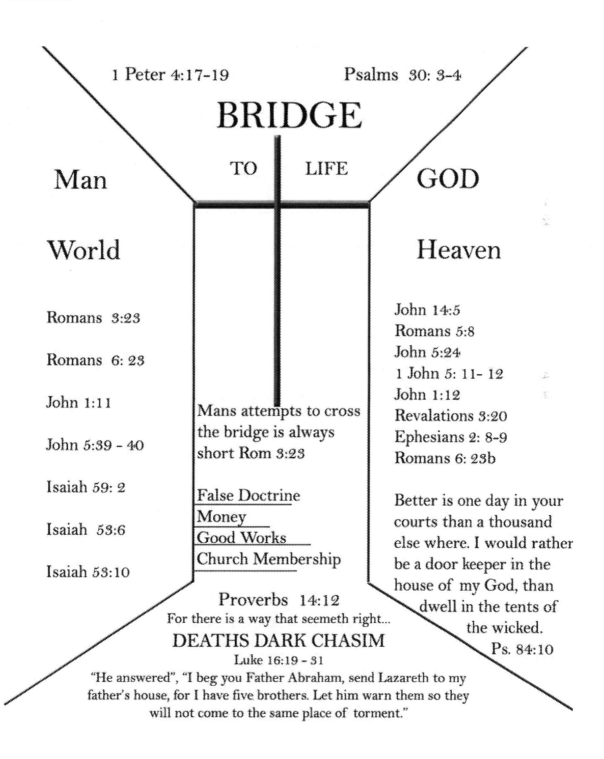

1 Peter 4:17-19   Psalms 30: 3-4

BRIDGE

TO   LIFE

Man   GOD

World   Heaven

Romans 3:23   John 14:5
                                                    Romans 5:8
Romans 6: 23   John 5:24
                                                    1 John 5: 11- 12
John 1:11   John 1:12
                                                    Revalations 3:20
John 5:39 - 40   Ephesians 2: 8-9
                                                    Romans 6: 23b

Isaiah 59: 2   Mans attempts to cross
                            the bridge is always   Better is one day in your
Isaiah 53:6   short Rom 3:23   courts than a thousand
                                                                  else where. I would rather
                            False Doctrine   be a door keeper in the
Isaiah 53:10   Money   house of my God, than
                            Good Works   dwell in the tents of
                            Church Membership   the wicked.

Proverbs 14:12   Ps. 84:10
For there is a way that seemeth right...
DEATHS DARK CHASIM
Luke 16:19 - 31
"He answered", "I beg you Father Abraham, send Lazareth to my
father's house, for I have five brothers. Let him warn them so they
will not come to the same place of torment."

Chapter 13

The Vine

It is no longer I who live, but Christ Who lives in me.

He Is The Vine, We Are The Branches

For when I tried to keep the law, it condemned me. So I died to the law—I stopped trying to meet all its requirements—so that I might live for God. **Galatians 2:19**

Reaching For Righteousness…..In The Light Of The Son. No one should stop obeying God, but they certainly need Christ to support them by His body and blood

John 7 People are prone to live for themselves. Not many lived for Jesus.

John 15:5 Be connected to Jesus all the time…for we can do nothing without Him.

Therefore, <u>let us offer through Jesus</u> a continual sacrifice of **praise to God**, proclaiming our allegiance to His name. And don't forget to do well and to share with those in need. These are the sacrifices that please God. **Hebrews 13:15-16**

Come along with me...Let's talk To this man from Galilee (Jesus)

Lord Jesus, I believe You!……..It is you alone, who knows my life like a book. Although I have lost most of the hair on my head, you know exactly how many were there before their departure. You know all things Lord, and completely know our reaction to all your intimate blessings and love that you send our way. I want to remain near you, Lord. Allow me to draw still closer to you. I believe your bible is true, and by being drawn closer to your word, I can walk with you, and become more like you. Let your word dwell richly in my heart and life for your glory, so I can be a better witness to the people in and around my life. Give me such things as your awareness reflects my needs. Please let me share with my friends and loved ones, even strangers, so that by sharing in the spirit with them, they too will become your child.

The winds are blowing and the rains are coming, but tuck these words in your heart and Treasure them…Never let them go….Words of love and praise.

How can a young person stay pure?
By obeying your word, I have tried hard to find you—
don't let me wander from your commands.
I have hidden your word in my heart,
that I might not sin against you. **Psalm 119:9-11**

Here are the results of such a person:

Jesus shouted to the crowds, "If you trust me, you are trusting not only me, but also God who sent me. For when you see me, you are seeing the one who sent me. I have come as a light to shine in this dark world, so that all who put their trust in me will no longer remain in the dark. **John 12:44-46**

Doesn't this light up the teaching in 2 Corinthians 5:17…..Be very sure to read this verse…. Ask yourself if this has happened to you. It is the very most important verse that Jesus has shared with us.

He Is The Vine, We Are The Branches

Can we produce grapes without nourishment?

Faith-The Holy Spirit--And You

Reaching For Righteousness…..In The Light Of The Son

John 7:16-18 Teach what comes from God. Jesus did.

John15:5 We can do nothing without Him.

Therefore, let us offer through Jesus a continual sacrifice of praise to God, proclaiming our allegiance to His name. And don't forget to do well and to share with those in need. These are the sacrifices that please God. **Hebrews 13:15-16**

The Vine And His Teaching Mission

Jesus did not come into the world to seek the praise of men, but to please His Father. Do you want to please the Father? Follow Jesus! He will take you to His Throne. I love to lead people through His Word, and especially to this room where he is living and waiting for you now.

Faith Builder….. "Why did you doubt?" Matthew 14:31

Let our faith and our commitment continue or begin here.

The Bible is God's Home ….Every book in the bible is the street where He is living, and every verse in the Bible is the room where He lives. Ever present . …..The room He is dwelling in is for your particular need. Thus, you are never without Him according to your own faith and needs. He always rejoices when you call on Him. Then He transfers that joy to your own heart. Oh, what a Savior, and who can live without him….Not one single person in all the world can live without Him……………**Check it out with John 15:5**

"I know all the things you do, that you are neither hot nor cold. I wish that you were one or the other! But since you are like lukewarm water, neither hot nor cold, I will spit you out of my mouth! You say, 'I am *rich.*' I have everything I want. I don't need a thing!' And you don't realize that you are wretched and miserable and poor and blind and naked. So I advise you to buy gold from me—gold that has been purified by fire. Then you will be rich. Also buy white garments from me so you will not be shamed by your nakedness, and ointment for your eyes so you will be able to see. I correct and discipline everyone I love. So be diligent and turn from your indifference.

"Look! I stand at the door and knock. If you hear my voice and open the door, I will come in, and we will share a meal together as friends. Those who are victorious will sit with me on my throne, just as I was victorious and sat with my Father on his throne. "Anyone with ears to hear must listen to the Spirit and understand what he is saying to the churches." Then, as I heard Jesus say, "Go call the others, so that My Father's House will be full." If they should ask, tell them, 'I Am' sent you.

Revelation 3:15-2

What Must You Do To Find Your Life In Christ? It Isn't As Hard As You May Think To Be Chosen. Choosing to follow Jesus is the joy of living.

Examine yourselves to see if your faith is genuine. Test yourselves. **Surely** you know that Jesus Christ is living in you; if not, you have failed the test of genuine faith. **2 Corinthians 13:5**

God gave us special gifts so that we could use them when He calls upon us to share His special message of hope and salvation. His gifts are very easy to use because we have His wisdom, direction and power when called upon. There are different kinds of gifts, but the same Spirit. There are different kinds of service, but the same Lord.

There are different kinds of working, but the same God works all of them in all men. Now to each one the manifestation of the Spirit is given for common good. A spiritual gift is given to each of us so we can help each other. To one person the Spirit gives the ability to give wise advice; to another the same Spirit gives a message of special knowledge. The same Spirit gives great faith to another, and to someone else the one Spirit gives the gift of healing. He gives one person the power to perform miracles, and another the ability to prophesy. He gives someone else the ability to discern whether a message is from the Spirit of God or from another spirit. Still another person is given the ability to speak in unknown languages, while another is given the ability to interpret what is being said. It is the one and only Spirit who distributes all these gifts. He alone decides which gift each person should have.

One Body with Many Parts:

The human body has many parts, but the many parts make up one whole body. So it is with the body of Christ. Some of us are Jews, some are Gentiles, some are slaves, and some are free. But we have all been baptized into one body by one Spirit, and we all share the same Spirit. Yes, the body has many different parts, not just one part.

1 Corinthians 4:1-5 explains in His loving ways how He calls me to ask: Have you found your gift, or the part of the body you belong to? You will want to take that special gift that He has given to you and lay it before Him when you finally see Him face to face.

Chapter 14

The Cornerstone
Of Faith
With

The Branch that bears much Fruit:

The Christian who is growing more like the Lord Jesus, is just like a real vine that must be cleaned from insects, mildew, and fungus, so the Christian must be cleansed from worldly things that cling to him. Even such vines need to be pruned or cleansed by the word at the time of conversion.

His word has a purifying effect on our lives. Teaching is only part of it; Immersing ourselves in his Word is of greater importance.

Matthew 14:27….Take courage ! It is I. Don't be Afraid. 'Come, He said.'

If thy word 'O Lord had not been my delight, I would have perished in my affliction. Psalm 119:92

You should explore and expand in the word of God, with the help and mercy of the Almighty. Trust the Holy Spirit to lead you.

Faith is seeing and obeying God's power in your life. If you don't see it, then search for it through His word.

He would not have sent Jesus, His only Son, to die in misery so that you could, or, would live without Him…..In a spirit of faith through His word…..(My faith assures me of that)

Who is Jesus, And what did He do for you? He brought 'Faith' greater than mere mental assent.

He is the Son of God and superior to angels. Everything that was made was made through Him. In the past God spoke to our forefathers through the prophets at many times and in various ways, but in these last days he has spoken to us by His Son, whom he appointed heir of all things, and through whom He made the universe. The Son is the radiance of God's glory and the exact representation of His being, sustaining all things by His powerful word. After He had provided purification for sins, He sat down at the right hand of the Majesty in Heaven. So He became as much superior to the angels as the name He has inherited is superior to theirs. For to which of the angels did God ever say, "You are my Son; Today I have become your Father. "Or again, "I will be His Father, And he will be my Son"? And again, when God brings his first borne into the world, he says, "Let all God's Angels worship Him.

"In speaking of the angels He say's, " He sends His angels like winds

His servants flames of fire." But about the Son He say's, "Your throne, O God, will last for ever and ever, and righteousness will be the scepter of Your Kingdom. You have loved righteousness and hated wickedness; Therefore God, your God, has set you above your companions by anointing you with the oil of joy."

He also says, "In the beginning, O Lord, you laid the foundations of the earth, And the heavens are the work of your hands. They will perish, but you remain; They will wear out like a garment. You will role them up like a robe; Like a garment they will be changed. But you remain the same, And your years will never end."To which of the angels did God ever say, "Sit at my right hand until I make your enemies a foot stool for your feet." **Hebrew 1:5-14**

Faith Builder..... "Why did you doubt?" Matthew 14:31

Let our faith and our commitment continue or begin here.

The bible is God's Home ....Every book in the bible is the street where He is living, and every verse in the bible is the room where He is staying. **Ever present . .....**The room He is dwelling in is for your particular need. Thus, you are never without Him according to your own faith and needs. **He always rejoices when you call on Him.** Then He transfers that joy to your own heart. **"Oh," what a Savior, and who can live without him....Not one single person in all the world.**

How, and why did God activate us?..... So we could be filled with his truth, obey it, and share it ?

Do you trust in your baptism, or, by Faith while walking with the Holy Spirit, and of being transformed into a new person? **(check out John 3:3)**

A Living Sacrifice to God

And so, dear brothers and sisters, I plead with you to give your bodies to God because of all He has done for you. Let them be a living and Holy sacrifice—the kind he will find acceptable. This is truly the way to worship Him. Don't copy the behavior and customs of this world, but let God transform you into a new person by changing the way you think. Then you will learn to know God's will for you, which is good and pleasing and perfect. He knew that I would believe it and then share it. He knew his Power would work in my life....That's why He created me, and that was known by Him before I was born. With these words we all find a purpose for our lives. We are touching base with faith now. But how does all His Power fill us each and every day ? Answer ?....Love and obedience ! His will before mine.

A fine subject for the rest of this book ! But let's just consider two words.....Love and obedience.

If I can love my life better without Him why should He control me? <u>Because the way I would live is the way of the flesh,</u> and the ways of the flesh we are told will perish.

Check it out

Don't you realize that your body is the temple of the Holy Spirit, who lives in you and was given to you by God? You do not belong to yourself, for God bought you with a high price. So you must honor God with your body. **1 Corinthians 6:19-20**

Any other process in our lives he calls rebellion because we haven't obeyed the call of His Son or decided to follow Him. Maybe we have made him our Savior, but we are controlling our ship. As He sits on the throne of our heart's we recognize and feel safe in his loving arms. When we place ourselves on the throne in our heart, he is no longer in control of your life.

Have you ever imagined being on a ship and you suddenly realize it has no captain...maybe someone threw him overboard. Then you instantly recognize a need for help as you see the person operating your ship with an unrecognizable badge. You wonder, can I trust him?

Then in an instant you flee to the friend you have in Jesus knowing it was you who left Him. What is next is to satisfy your guilty conscience and heart ? Repentance? A sudden renewal of your faith along with a thought 'I'm not doing that again.' Now we realize who let the strange captain be the guide of our destiny, leading us to sin. Then comes the love and longing for Jesus. The safety of his being near with instant promises. The faith of His promise that he will neither leave you or forsake you. What a friend we have in Jesus ! Jesus also said these words.

"I am the vine; you are the branches. If a man remains in me and I in him, he will bear much fruit; apart from me you can do nothing. **John 15:5**

My praise to the Father for letting us be brothers, <u>by connecting us with Jesus:</u>

So it is right that I should feel as I do about all of you, **for you have a special place in my heart.** You share with me the special favor of God, both in my imprisonment and in defending and confirming the truth of the Good News. God knows how much I love you and long for you with the tender compassion of Christ Jesus. I pray that your love will overflow more and more, and that you will keep on growing in knowledge and understanding. For I want you to understand what really matters, so that you may live pure and blameless lives until the day of Christ's return. May you always be filled with the fruit of your salvation—the righteous character produced in your life by Jesus Christ—for this will bring much glory and praise to God.

Paul's Joy was knowing That Christ Is Preached.

"And I want you to know, my dear brothers and sisters, that everything that has happened to me here has helped to spread the Good News. For everyone here, including the whole palace guard, knows that I am in chains because of Christ. And because of my imprisonment, most of the believers here have gained confidence and boldly speak God's message without fear.

It's true that some are preaching out of jealousy and rivalry. But others preach about Christ with pure motives. They preach because they love me, for they know I have been appointed to defend the Good News. Those others do not have pure motives as they preach about Christ. They preach with selfish ambition, not sincerely, intending to make my chains more painful to me. But that doesn't matter. Whether their motives are false or genuine, the message about Christ is being preached either way, so I rejoice. And I will continue to rejoice. For I know that as you pray for me and the Spirit of Jesus Christ helps me, this will lead to my deliverance."

Paul's Life in Christ

For I fully expect and hope that I will never be ashamed, but that I will continue to be bold for Christ, as I have been in the past. And I trust that my life will bring honor to Christ, whether I live or die. For to me, living means living for Christ, and dying is even better. But if I live, I can do more fruitful work for Christ. So I really don't know which is better. I'm torn between two desires: I long to go and be with Christ, which would be far better for me. But for your sakes, it is better that I continue to live.

Philippians 1:1-26 Knowing this, I am convinced that I will remain alive so I can continue to help all of you grow and experience the joy of your faith. And when I come to you again, you will have even more reason to take pride in Christ Jesus because of what he is doing through me. Let these thoughts permeate your heart if you haven't yet received Him As your Lord, God and Savior.

Today I am 77 years old. Yesterday I was only 18, at least it seems that way. At any rate, life moves along at a pretty steady pace, and each day without Christ is lost. My heart was filled with it's joy of each day's happenings. I had no knowledge of a personal relationship with Christ until I reached the age of 42. I had no experience of the happy times in Christ. He waited while I wasted my time in the pleasures of the world, mired in sin.

I was fortunately blessed in such an undeserving manner with a family of nine including myself. He blessed us with seven beautiful children. Their lives without a 'Saved' Father or

Mother, were lifeless in the Spirit until Christ came bursting onto the scene after our fifth child, all boy's. While our two girls were in the waiting room. Instantly we were around the kitchen table studying portals of prayer while offering individual prayers among us. Two years later I was saved (I was rather dense as to what his plans were for my life, and the remaining eight family members) yet true faith was always God's plan from beginning to end............ I include this little paragraph to say, "I wasted many of my days and nights, and the lives of other family members, in a life that could have been filled with praises to our Lord and Savior 'with joy overflowing'!"

Philippians 4:6-9 In Philippians we read don't worry about anything; instead, pray about everything. Tell God what you need, and thank Him for all He has done. Then you will experience God's peace, which exceeds anything we can understand. His peace will guard your hearts and minds as you live in Christ Jesus.

And now, dear brothers and sisters, one final thing. Fix your thoughts on what is true, and honorable, and right, and pure, and lovely, and admirable. Think about things that are excellent and worthy of praise. Keep putting into practice all you learned and received from me—everything you heard from me and saw me doing. Then the God of peace will be with you.

Editorial note: Even as I try diligently to emulate Christ, the 'me' in the text are the words of The Apostle Paul.

A Faith that Lives Without the weight of worldly issues.

Philippians 3:7-11 I once thought all these things were so very important, but now I consider them worthless because of what Christ has done. Yes, everything else is worthless when compared with the priceless gain of knowing Christ Jesus my Lord. I have discarded everything else, counting it all as garbage, so that I may have Christ and become one with him. I no longer count on my own goodness or my ability to obey God's law, but I trust Christ to save me. For God's way of making us right with Himself depends on faith. As a result, I can really know Christ and experience the Mighty Power that raised Him from the dead. I can learn what it means to suffer with Him, sharing in His death, so that, somehow, I can experience the resurrection from the dead!

With this command I challenge you to.... GO! Share His Message With all His Blessings. Yes, Indeed. Go!

God's design is for us to be radical Christian's, passionately in love with Him. He is a jealous God and will not settle for second place.

The Law and Faith in Christ:

Oh, foolish Galatians! Who has cast an evil spell on you? For the meaning of Jesus Christ's death was made as clear to you as if you had seen a picture of his death on the cross. Let me ask you this one question: Did you receive the Holy Spirit by obeying the law of Moses? Of course not! You received the Spirit because you believed the message you heard about Christ. How foolish can you be? After starting your Christian lives in the Spirit, why are you now trying to become perfect by your own human effort? Have you experienced so much for nothing? Surely it was not in vain, was it? I ask you again, does God give you the Holy Spirit and work miracles among you because you obey the law? Of course not! It is because you believe the message you heard about Christ. In the same way, "Abraham believed God, and God counted him as righteous because of his faith." **Galatians 3:1-7**

The real children of Abraham, then, are those who put their faith in God. *What's more, the Scriptures looked forward to this time when God would declare the Gentiles to be righteous because of their faith. God proclaimed this good news to Abraham long ago when he said, "All nations will be blessed through you." So all who put their faith in Christ share the same blessing Abraham received because of his faith.*

But those who depend on the law to make them right with God are under his curse, for the Scriptures say, "Cursed is everyone who does not observe and obey all the commands that are written in God's Book of the Law." So it is clear that no one can be made right with God by trying to keep the law. For the Scriptures say, "It is through faith that a righteous person has life." This way of faith is very different from the way of law, which says, "It is through obeying the law that a person has life." But Christ has rescued us from the curse pronounced by the law. When he was hung on the cross, he took upon himself the curse for our wrongdoing. For it is written in the Scriptures, "Cursed is everyone who is hung on a tree." Through Christ Jesus, God has blessed the Gentiles with the same blessing he promised to Abraham, so that we who are believers might receive the promised Holy Spirit through faith.

The Law and God's Promise Dear brothers and sisters, here's an example from everyday life. Just as no one can set aside or amend an irrevocable agreement, so it is in this case. God gave the promises to Abraham and his child. And notice that the Scripture doesn't say "to his children," as if it meant many descendants. Rather, it says "to his child"—and that, of course, means Christ. This is what I am trying to say: The agreement God made with Abraham could not be canceled 430 years later when God gave the law to Moses. God would be breaking his promise. For if the inheritance could be received by keeping the law, then it would not be the result of accepting God's promise. But God graciously gave it to Abraham as a promise. Why, then, was the law given? It was given alongside the promise to show people their sins. But the law was designed to last only until the coming of the child who was promised. God gave his law through angels to Moses, who was the mediator between God and the people. Now a mediator is helpful if more than one party must reach an agreement. But God, who is one, did not use a mediator when he gave his promise to Abraham.

Is there a conflict, then, between God's law and God's promises? Absolutely not! If the law could give us new life, we could be made right with God by obeying it. But the Scriptures declare that we are all prisoners of sin, so we receive God's promise of freedom only by believing in Jesus Christ, inviting Him into our hearts, with an urgency.

Jesus didn't come to abolish the law. He came to fulfill it for us, so that by faith in Him, we could be found in Him as we live in this earthly tent. He in us and we in Him. Have you invited Him into your heart and life yet. If so, your sins are nailed to the cross and you and your sins died with Him. There is nothing but pure undefiled joy within your heart and life. He put it there to identify you as His very own.

God's Children through Faith

Before the way of faith in Christ was available to us, we were placed under guard by the law. We were kept in protective custody, so to speak, until the way of faith was revealed. Let me put it another way. The law was our guardian until Christ came; it protected us until we could be made right with God through faith. And now that the way of faith has come, we no longer need the law as our guardian.

For you are all children of God through faith in Christ Jesus. And all who have been united with Christ in baptism have put on Christ, like putting on new clothes. There is no longer Jew or Gentile slave or free, male and female. For you are all one in Christ Jesus. And now that you belong to Christ, you are the true children of Abraham. You are His heirs, and God's promise to Abraham belongs to you. So ends chapter three of Galatians. **Romans 4:9-25**

Chapter 15

The Beatitudes
The values of His teachings:

"God blesses those who realize their need for Him,

for the Kingdom of Heaven is given to them.

God blesses those who mourn,

for they will be comforted.

God blesses those who are gentle and lowly,

for the whole earth will belong to them

God blesses those who are hungry and thirsty for justice,

for they will receive it in full.

God blesses those who are merciful,

for they will be shown mercy.

God blesses those whose hearts are pure,

for they will see God.

God blesses those who work for peace,

for they will be called the children of God.

God blesses those who are persecuted because they live for God,

for the Kingdom of Heaven is theirs.

"God blesses you when you are mocked and persecuted and lied about because you are my followers. Be happy about it! Be very glad! For a

great reward awaits you in heaven. And remember, the Ancient Prophets were persecuted, too. **Matthew 5:3–10**

Chapter 16

Chosen Life Study Testimonials

From The Pautsch Family

To the ends of the earth.

Rooted and Built up in Him; Steadfast In the faith as you were taught…. And overflowing with Thanksgiving. **Colossians 2:7**

I personally met Bob when I visited my parents in the late 70's, and really got to know Bob when I moved to DeWitt with my new bride in 1980. Bob always loved to talk about Jesus, and his life was usually filled with testimonies and stories of people he had been talking to about their relationship with Christ and their salvation. Bob persisted in his evangelistic fervor. He was a great source of motivation as I saw his unbridled enthusiasm and emotion for the Lord.

When unbelieving folks in the church persecuted my father in 1991-1992 Bob stood like the Rock of Gibraltar, standing up for righteousness and speaking of knowing Jesus to the persecutors.

Bob is like the people mentioned in Hebrews 11…of whom the world in not worthy!

With Bob's love of evangelism it's easy to understand how the following verse applies to Bob, "Ah, Sovereign Lord," I said, "I do not know how to speak; I am only a child." But the Lord said to me, "Do not say, 'I am only a child.' You must go to everyone I send you to and say whatever I command you. Do not be afraid of them, for I am with you and will rescue you," declares the Lord. **Jeremiah 1:6–8**

My Father was the Pastor in the DeWitt, Iowa church that Bob was attending around the time when his close encounter with death occurred. When my parents moved to DeWitt Bob was one of the first people to introduce himself. In fact, one of his first comments to my parents knit their hearts together with Bob's when he said, "I don't know if you understand this but ever since my accident I've had such a strong love for Jesus." They quickly affirmed that they surely knew where he was coming from. Bob's following comment was endearing when he said, "Since you moved to DeWitt the atmosphere has been clearer for miles because it's clear that you love Jesus too."

Over the 16 years that my father was pastor in DeWitt, Bob was always a great source of encouragement and a faithful witness for Jesus. This thrilled my father more than anything since my dad had such a great passion to make certain that people knew the Gospel. There was never a sermon that went by that my dad didn't include the expression, "God loves you so much He sent Jesus to die for your sins." Bob and my dad shared this passion for the Gospel and this certainly explains their close relationship as well as the abundant fruit that has come out of their lives.

Our Lord Jesus called my Father home to be with Him on January 1, 2000—Y2K Day! He just made it into the 2000's. My mother and I were there at his bedside when he left his earth suit and was ushered by the angels into heaven. He would have been 75 on May 10, 2000. He left behind a multitude of redeemed souls thrilled by the Gospel and his faithfulness to preaching it. It's a real testimony to my dad how many people have shared of their love for him and told of their appreciation for his dedication to Christ and his life of integrity.

Thanks for your expressions of love, Bob. You're a dear soul and, through the thick and the thin, you have never wavered in your commitment to Jesus. I'm sure you have given, and are giving, the Lord great pleasure!

David Pautsch

Praise Our Glorious Lord

Thanks David and to all the ministers of His Word, their Wives and all who witnessed His Glorious name including my son Douglas, along with the rest of our family who are fighting the good fight.

In Jesus Glorious Love,

Bob

It is a wonderful experience to have friendship in the Lord and to know that as time passes by and miles upon miles separate.....spiritual friendships remain. Bob and Sylvia are two special people that I have had the privilege of knowing and spending time with sharing about the marvelous experience of life when we walk with the Lord. Bob's personal sharing of his encounters with God and the way God has been at work in his life are precious. His spiritual love for his family and friends goes beyond natural friendship. The reflections Bob shares with us are indicative of a man in love with His Master and intent upon sharing the goodness of God with others. I know you will enjoy it as a devotional blessing.

Warmly

Pastor
Tim and Cynthia McClellan

Eric & Jodi Sloter

As Bob's former pastor, it is my joy to share Christ, His Word and His Way, with my friend and brother, Bob Bowman. While Bob and I do not see each other as often as we have in past years, we both celebrate that in Christ our friendship is eternal.

And so, with eternity in mind, I pray with you, Bob, that your book, "A Chosen Life Study," will reach those who are yet to hear and respond to the good news of Christ in our world today. I trust with confidence that the Lord's anointing on your first book will carry this book to the ends of the earth. May the Lord Himself speed onward your mission to reach others for Christ and may your life and your book in every way reflect the true and life transforming glory of the very Son of God, the Lord Jesus Christ.

Through Christ Jesus our Lord with joy!

Eric Sloter
Lead Pastor.....Cedar Valley Community Church

Doug Bowman

I am not a writer, dad, but you ask me if I would represent Wartburg College in the back section of your book A Chosen Life. So, because you have been so formidable in leading me and your other six children to Christ, I find myself elated at the opportunity to not only represent Wartburg College in my witness of Christ, but also you, dad, in your book A Chosen Life Study. It has been your life in terms of your spiritual make-up. After having my paralyzing stroke six months ago, in 2005, I understand more clearly what a blessing it is to

143

be able to walk with Jesus. After graduating from high school I never realized there would be a time of renewal, when Christ would again be so important in my life. Fellowship with Jesus is the core of life, and sometimes He teaches us that the hard way. I had not experienced what a "New Life" was, in the body or in the spirit. My stroke brought about a physical change as I encountered the many limitations to my daily routine. One of the great blessings of that is the small whisper of God when He says "Be still, and know that I am God" Psalm 46:10.

I have also been lifted through my new excitement in life as I experience Him spiritually, very much like you when you experienced a near death situation in your own life while we were all growing up in the years of our youth.

I am so grateful to Jesus that He would bring our lives back together like He promised in John 10:9-10 where He tells us: Yes, I am the gate. Those who come in through me will be saved. Wherever they go, they will find green pastures. The thief's purpose is to steal and kill and destroy. My purpose is to give life in all its fullness.

I pray that your book A Chosen Life Study will draw many to the wonderful experience and the blessings of God through His Son Jesus Christ.

Chapter 17

Something personal

My Cup

I didn't search for riches, nor dream of them just now,

Contentment has always led me, to be happy anyhow…

I've gone along life's journey, reaping more than I have sowed

And I'm drinking from my saucer, cause my cup has overflowed…

I have many family riches, when the going seems so tough,

And holding to the families love in Christ, has made me rich enough…

Just thanking God for blessings, and the mercies He's bestowed,

Finds me drinking from my saucer, Cause my cup has overflowed…

Remembering times when things went wrong, recalling faith so thin,

As I watched the dark clouds rolling by, the Son came back again…

So I asked the Lord to forgive my gripe, 'bout the tough rows I had hoed

Then thanked Him for the saucer, cause my cup has overflowed…

He gives me strength and courage, as the way grows steep and tough,

Should I ask for extra blessings, when I know I've had enough?

May I never be too busy, to help others with their load,

And offer them my cup, because mine has overflowed…

Poem by Bob Bowman

I have learned the secret of contentment, whether it is with a full stomach or empty, with plenty or little. For I can do everything with the help of Christ who gives me the strength I need. **Philippians 4:11-13**

The Bible is God's Home ….Every book in the Bible is the street where He is living, and every verse in the bible is the room where He lives. Ever present …...The room He is dwelling in, is for your particular need. Thus, you are never without Him according to your own faith and needs. He always rejoices when you call on Him. Then He transfers that joy to your own heart. Ooooh, what a Savior, and who can live without him….Not one single person in all the world.

Confess your sins to each other and pray for each other so that you may be healed. The earnest prayer of a righteous person has great power and produces wonderful results. **James 5:1**

Poem Based on 2 Corinthians 13:5

I looked for the sin of un-forgiveness, to see if my heart had a clue,

Especially a sign that would focus, any harm I was holding 'gainst you…

And there I found the Lord Jesus, ready to speak love so rare,

I said 'Lord forgive my bitterness, still give me your passion to share'…

My heart cries out for your mercy, in the sensitive eyes of your love,

I can't help but know of your mercy, your voice is so loving above…

Nor can I help, 'but know your forgiveness', despite the hurts in my life,

You cover my wounds so depressing, lingering long in my strife…

Yet while I tune out the yesterdays', calling your Spirit on high,

To muffle the sound of my aching heart, and changing the sound of my cry…

Would you help me again to tell others, 'bout your mercy in forgiving my sin'?

As I lift up your name to the heavens, as I carry your life from within…

Poem by Bob Bowman

A Name Above All Names has Called You To be Like Him…

If You Have Answered…..

You are a new creation of Infinite worth

You Are Deeply Loved

You Are Completely Forgiven By Him

You Are Truly Pleasing to Him

You Are Truly Accepted Through Him

You are Absolutely Complete In Him

You were Chosen For Fellowship With Him

Before Time Began God Purposed Your Life

He Made You Special. And He Paid The Price!

This Is your Book: To gain more of His knowledge, Wisdom and understanding, put your name on this line for His glory; and for that reason surrender, or reconfirm that you have surrendered to Him.

Your Name_____

God Offers Comfort to All

All praise to God, the Father of our Lord Jesus Christ. God is our merciful Father and the source of all comfort. He comforts us in all our troubles so that we can comfort others. When they are troubled, we will be able to give them the same comfort God has given us. For the more we suffer for Christ, the more God will shower us with his comfort through Christ. Even when we are weighed down with troubles, it is for your comfort and salvation! For when we ourselves are comforted, we will certainly comfort you. Then you can patiently endure the same things we suffer. We are confident that as you share in our sufferings, you will also share in the comfort God gives us.

 We think you ought to know, dear brothers and sisters,[b] about the trouble we went through in the province of Asia. We were crushed and overwhelmed beyond our ability to endure, and we thought we would never live through it. In fact, we expected to die. But as a result, we stopped relying on ourselves and learned to rely only on God, who raises the dead. And he did rescue us from mortal danger, and he will rescue us again. We have placed our confidence in him, and he will continue to rescue us. And you are helping us by praying for us. Then many people will give thanks because God has graciously answered so many prayers for our safety.

Paul's Change of Plans

We can say with confidence and a clear conscience that we have lived with a God-given holiness and sincerity in all our dealings. We have depended on God's grace, not on our own human wisdom. That is how we have conducted ourselves before the world, and especially toward you. Our letters have been straightforward, and there is nothing written between the lines and nothing you can't understand. I hope someday you will fully understand us, even if you don't understand us now. Then on the day when the Lord Jesus returns, you will be proud of us in the same way we are proud of you.

Since I was so sure of your understanding and trust, I wanted to give you a double blessing by visiting you twice— first on my way to Macedonia and again when I returned from Macedonia. Then you could send me on my way to Judea.

You may be asking why I changed my plan. Do you think I make my plans carelessly? Do you think I am like people of the world who say "Yes" when they really mean "No"? As surely as God is faithful, my word to you does not waver between "Yes" and "No." For Jesus Christ, the Son of God, does not waver between "Yes" and "No." He is the one whom Silas, Timothy, and I preached to you, and as God's ultimate "Yes," he always does what he says. For all of God's promises have been fulfilled in Christ with a resounding "Yes!" And through Christ, our "Amen" (which means "Yes") ascends to God for his glory.

It is God who enables us, along with you, to stand firm for Christ. He has commissioned us, and he has identified us as his own by placing the Holy Spirit in our hearts as the first installment that guarantees everything he has promised us.

Now I call upon God as my witness that I am telling the truth. The reason I didn't return to Corinth was to spare you from a severe rebuke. But that does not mean we want to dominate you by telling you how to put your faith into practice. We want to work together with you so you will be full of joy, for it is by your own faith that you stand firm. **2 Corinthians 1:3-23**

Nehemiah 8:10 Nehemiah said, "Go and enjoy some good food and sweet drinks. Send some of it to those who don't have any. This day is set apart to honor our Lord. So don't be sad. <u>The joy of the Lord makes you strong.</u>"

John 15:11 I have told you this so that my joy will be in you. I also want your joy to be complete.

Mathew 25:21 "His master replied, 'You have done well, good and faithful servant! You have been faithful with a few things. I will put you in charge of many things. Come and share your master's happiness!'

<u>Isaiah29:13-19</u> The Lord says, "These people worship me only with their words.
They honor me by what they say. But their hearts are far away from me.
Their worship doesn't mean anything to me.
<u>They teach nothing but human rules.</u>

So once more I will shock these people with many wonderful acts.
I will destroy the wisdom of those who think they are so wise.
I will do away with the cleverness of those who think they are so smart."
How terrible it will be for people who do everything they can
to hide their plans from the Lord! They do their work in darkness.
They think, "Who sees us? Who will know?" They turn everything upside down. How silly they are to think that potters are like the clay they work with!
Can what is made say to the one who made it,
"You didn't make me"? Can the pot say to the potter,

"You don't know anything"? In a very short time, Lebanon will be turned into rich farm lands. The rich farm lands will seem like a forest.

At that time those who can't hear will hear what is read from the scroll.

Those who are blind will come out of gloom and darkness. They will be able to see. 19 Those who aren't proud will once again find their joy in the Lord.

And those who are in need will find their joy in the Holy One of Israel.

Psalm 30:5 His anger lasts for only a moment. But his favor lasts for a person's whole life. Sobbing can remain through the night.

But joy comes in the morning.

Chapter 18

"The Heart"

...His Heart...

Or Our Hearts

Will we Lead....Follow...Or Fall

My heart is burdened <u>for all who took the time to read</u> "A Chosen Life Study." I am praying as I close this book with God speaking through me that the scriptures He shared with me would sink deep into your hearts where each word will refresh and bring you alive to His will. I wanted to close with a chapter that will awaken all of us to what the Apostle Paul went through to bring us life in Christ.....

In **John 1:4** Jesus said these words: "<u>In Him (Jesus) was Life, and that Life was the Light of men.</u>"

Followed by 2 Corinthians 2:1-17

So I decided that I would not bring you grief with another painful visit.

For if I cause you grief, who will make me glad? Certainly not someone I have grieved. That is why I wrote to you as I did, so that when I do come, I won't be grieved by the very ones who ought to give me the greatest joy. Surely you all know that my joy comes from your being joyful. I wrote that letter in great anguish, with a troubled heart and many tears. I didn't want to grieve you, but I wanted to let you know how much love I have for you.

Forgiveness for the Sinner

I am not overstating it when I say that the man who caused all the trouble hurt all of you more than he hurt me. Most of you opposed him, and that was punishment enough.

Now, however, it is time to forgive and comfort him. Otherwise he may be overcome by discouragement. So I urge you now to reaffirm your love for him.

I wrote to you as I did to test you and see if you would fully comply with my instructions. When you forgive this man, I forgive him, too. And when I forgive whatever needs to be forgiven, I do so with Christ's authority for your benefit, so that Satan will not outsmart us. For we are familiar with his evil schemes.

When I came to the city of Troas to preach the Good News of Christ, the Lord opened a door of opportunity for me. But I had no peace of mind because my dear brother Titus hadn't yet arrived with a report from you. So I said good-bye and went on to Macedonia to find him.

Ministers of the New Covenant

But thank God! He has made us his captives and continues to lead us along in Christ's triumphal procession. Now he uses us to spread the knowledge of Christ everywhere, like a sweet perfume. Our lives are a Christ-like fragrance rising up to God. But this fragrance is perceived differently by those who are being saved and by those who are perishing. To those who are perishing, we are a dreadful smell of death and doom. But to those who are being saved, we are a life-giving perfume. And who is adequate for such a task as this?

You see, we are not like the many hucksters[a] who preach for personal profit. We preach the word of God with sincerity and with Christ's authority, knowing that God is watching us. **2 Corinthians 2:1-17**

Revelation 21:1-27

A New Heaven and a New Earth

1. Then I saw "a new heaven and a new earth, for the first heaven and the first earth had passed away, and there was no longer any sea. 2. I saw the Holy City, the new Jerusalem, coming down out of heaven from God, prepared as a bride beautifully dressed for her husband. 3. And I heard a loud voice from the throne saying, "Look! God's dwelling place is now among the people, and he will dwell with them. They will be his people, and God himself will be with them and be their God. 4. 'He will wipe every tear from their eyes. There will be no more death' or mourning or crying or pain, for the old order of things has passed away."

5. He who was seated on the throne said, "I am making everything new! Then he said, "Write this down, for these words are trustworthy and true."

6. He said to me: "It is done. I am the Alpha and the Omega, the Beginning and the End. To the thirsty I will give water without cost from the spring of the water of life. 7. Those who are

victorious will inherit all this, and I will be their God and they will be my children. [8.] But the cowardly, the unbelieving, the vile, the murderers, the sexually immoral, those who practice magic arts, the idolaters and all liars—they will be consigned to the fiery lake of burning sulfur. This is the second death."

The New Jerusalem, the Bride of the Lamb

[9.] One of the seven angels who had the seven bowls full of the seven last plagues came and said to me, "Come, I will show you the bride, the wife of the Lamb." [10.] And he carried me away in the Spirit to a mountain great and high, and showed me the Holy City, Jerusalem, coming down out of heaven from God. [11.] It shone with the glory of God, and its brilliance was like that of a very precious jewel, like a jasper, clear as crystal. [12.] It had a great, high wall with twelve gates, and with twelve angels at the gates. On the gates were written the names of the twelve tribes of Israel. [13.] There were three gates on the east, three on the north, three on the south and three on the west. [14.] The wall of the city had twelve foundations, and on them were the names of the twelve apostles of the Lamb.

[15.] The angel who talked with me had a measuring rod of gold to measure the city, its gates and its walls. [16.] The city was laid out like a square, as long as it was wide. He measured the city with the rod and found it to be 12,000 stadia in length, and as wide and high as it is long. [17.] He measured its wall and it was 144 cubits thick, by human measurement, which the angel was using. [18.] The wall was made of jasper, and the city of pure gold, as pure as glass. [19.] The foundations of the city walls were decorated with every kind of precious stone. The first foundation was jasper, the second sapphire, the third agate, the fourth emerald, [20.] the fifth onyx, the sixth ruby, the seventh chrysolite, the eighth beryl, the ninth topaz, the tenth turquoise, the eleventh jacinth, and the twelfth amethyst. [21.] The twelve gates were twelve pearls, each gate made of a single pearl. The great street of the city was of gold, as pure as transparent glass.

[22.] I did not see a temple in the city, because the Lord God Almighty and the Lamb are its temple. [23.] The city does not need the sun or the moon to shine on it, for the glory of God gives it light, and the Lamb is its lamp. [24.] The nations will walk by its light, and the kings of the earth will bring their splendor into it. [25.] On no day will its gates ever be shut, for there will be no night there. [26.] The glory and honor of the nations will be brought into it. [27.] Nothing impure will ever enter it, nor will anyone who does what is shameful or deceitful, but only those whose names are written in the Lamb's book of life.

The Priestly Prayer

John 17

Jesus Prays

[1]After Jesus had finished speaking to his disciples, he looked up toward heaven and prayed:

Father, the time has come for you to bring glory to your Son, in order that he may bring glory to you. [2]And you gave him power over all people, so that he would give eternal life to everyone you give him. [3]Eternal life is to know you, the only true God, and to know Jesus Christ, the one you sent. [4]I have brought glory to you here on earth by doing everything you gave me to do. [5]Now, Father, give me back the glory that I had with you before the world was created.

[6]You have given me some followers from this world, and I have shown them what you are like. They were yours, but you gave them to me, and they have obeyed you. [7]They know that you gave me everything I have. [8]I told my followers what you told me, and they accepted it. They know that I came from you, and they believe that you are the one who sent me. [9]I am praying for them, but not for those who belong to this world. [a] My followers belong to you, and I am praying for them. [10]All that I have is yours, and all that you have is mine, and they will bring glory to me. [11]Holy Father, I am no longer in the world. I am coming to you, but my followers are still in the world. So keep them safe by the power of the name that you have given me. Then they will be one with each other, just as you and I are one. [12]While I was with them, I kept them safe by the power you have given me. I guarded them, and not one of them was lost, except the one who had to be lost. This happened so that what the Scriptures say would come true.

[13]I am on my way to you. But I say these things while I am still in the world, so that my followers will have the same complete joy that I do. [14]I have told them your message. But the people of this world hate them, because they don't belong to this world, just as I don't.

[15]Father, I don't ask you to take my followers out of the world, but keep them safe from the evil one. [16]They don't belong to this world, and neither do I. [17]Your word is the truth. So let this truth make them completely yours. [18]I am sending them into the world, just as you sent me. [19]I have given myself completely for their sake, so that they may belong completely to the truth.

[20]I am not praying just for these followers. I am also praying for everyone else who will have faith because of what my followers will say about me. [21]I want all of them to be one with each other, just as I am one with you and you are one with me. I also want them to be one with us. Then the people of this world will believe that you sent me.

[22]I have honored my followers in the same way that you honored me, in order that they may be one with each other, just as we are one. [23]I am one with them, and you are one with me, so that they may become completely one. Then this world's people will know that you sent me. They will know that you love my followers as much as you love me.

²⁴Father, I want everyone you have given me to be with me, wherever I am. Then they will see the glory that you have given me, because you loved me before the world was created. ²⁵Good Father, the people of this world don't know you. But I know you, and my followers know that you sent me. ²⁶I told them what you are like, and I will tell them even more. Then the love that you have for me will become part of them, and I will be one with them.

Love

1 Corinthians 13

If I speak in the tongues of men and of angels, but have not love, I am only a

Resounding gong or a clanging cymbal. If I have the gift of prophecy and can fathom all mysteries and all knowledge, and if I have a faith that can move mountains, but have

not love, I am nothing. If I give all I possess to the poor and surrender my body to the

flames, but have not love, I gain nothing.

Love is patient, love is kind. It does not envy, it does not boast, it is not proud. It is not

rude, it is not self-seeking, it is not easily angered, it keeps no record of wrongs. Love

does not delight in evil but rejoices with the truth. It always protects, always trusts,

always hopes, always perseveres.

Love never fails. But where there are prophecies, they will cease; where there are

tongues, they will be stilled; where there is knowledge, it will pass away. For we know in

part and we prophesy in part, but when perfection comes, the imperfect disappears.

When I was a child, I talked like a child, I thought like a child, I reasoned like a child.

When I became a man, I put childish ways behind me. Now we see but a poor reflection

as in a mirror; then we shall see face to face. Now I know in part; then I shall know

fully, even as I am fully known. And now these three remain: faith, hope and love. But the greatest of these is love.

They continued steadfastly in the apostles' doctrine and fellowship, in the breaking of bread, and in prayers (Acts 2:42).

Perhaps you thought you had "arrived" when you became a Christian. And in a sense you had!

You arrived at the starting line of a race—a race to be "continued steadfastly"—as the first converts to Christianity learned (2:42).

A. W. Tozer echoes this theme into his insightful look at conversion—an event that the Bible portrays more as a place to start than to finish.

Walk with A. W. Tozer

"Conversion for the early Christians was not a destination; it was the beginning of a journey.

"And right there is often where the biblical emphasis differs from our own.

"In our eagerness to make converts, we allow our hearers to absorb the idea that they can deal with their entire responsibility once and for all by an act of believing.

"In the book of Acts, faith was for each believer a beginning, not a bed in which to lie while waiting for the Lord's triumph.

"Believing was not a once-done act. It was an attitude of heart and mind which inspired and enabled the believer to follow the Lord wherever He went.

" 'They continued,' says Luke, and it is plain that only by continuing did they confirm their faith."

Walk Closer to God

Whether in the first century or the twenty first, the hope of heaven comes the same way—through our believing faith in the Savior.

That's "Step One" in the lifelong adventure of walking with God. But one step does not make a journey. Indeed, there are many steps to follow.

Instruction in the Word, fellowship with other believers, communication with the Father in prayer and worship (2:42)—each represents a step in the right direction.

And in the process of learning to walk, you'll discover that following the Lord is the only race in which you grow stronger with each step you take.

Not an end, but a beginning

Worship from the Heart

In the Old Testament, fire was used two ways: one, as a purifying agent to refine, purge, and burn away dross; two, as a symbol for an inner passion or a deep hunger for God. As you meditate on the appropriateness of fire as a symbol of the Holy Spirit, ask yourself which function is most needed in your life. As an act of worship, yield your life to Him, asking that He purify you and ignite your holy passion.

Walk Thru the Word

New Testament:
Acts 2

Old Testament:
Psalm 84:4-7

This devotion is used with the permission of Walk Through The Bible. It was used by them in their February 2, 2009 issue.

SPREAD HIS FAME SO EVERYONE WILL KNOW HIS SALVATION.

He will be one of your own people. You must listen to everything he tells you. Those who do not listen to him will be completely cut off from their people.

Deuteronomy 18:15,18,19

Acts 3

Peter Heals the Disabled Beggar

One day Peter and John were going up to the temple. It was three o'clock in the afternoon. It was the time for prayer. A man unable to walk was being carried to the temple gate called Beautiful. He had been that way since he was born. Every day someone put him near the gate. There he would beg from people going into the temple courtyards.

He saw that Peter and John were about to enter. So he asked them for money. Peter looked straight at him, and so did John. Then Peter said, "Look at us!" So the man watched them closely. He expected to get something from them.

Peter said, "I don't have any silver or gold. But I'll give you what I have. In the name of Jesus Christ of Nazareth, get up and walk." Then Peter took him by the right hand and helped him up. At once the man's feet and ankles became strong. He jumped to his feet and began to walk. He went with Peter and John into the temple courtyards. He walked and jumped and praised God. All the people saw him walking and praising God. They recognized him as the same man who used to sit and beg at the temple gate called Beautiful. (all Christians are beggars…Looking up to God almighty in the beautiful name of Jesus.) They were filled with wonder. They were amazed at what had happened to him.

Peter Speaks to the Jews

The beggar was holding on to Peter and John. All the people were amazed. They came running to them at Solomon's Porch. When Peter saw this, he said, "Men of Israel, why does this surprise you? Why do you stare at us? We haven't made this man walk by our own power or godliness. The God of our fathers, Abraham, Isaac and Jacob, has done this. He has brought glory to Jesus, who serves him. But you handed Jesus over to be killed. Pilate had decided to let him go. But you spoke against Jesus when he was in Pilate's court. You spoke against the Holy and Blameless One. You asked for a murderer to be set free instead. You killed the one who gives life. But God raised him from the dead. We are witnesses of this. This man whom you see and know was made strong because of faith in Jesus' name. Faith in Jesus has healed him completely. You can see it with your own eyes.

"My friends, I know you didn't realize what you were doing. Neither did your leaders. But God had given a promise through all the prophets. And this is how he has made his promise come true. He said that his Christ would suffer. So turn away from your sins. Turn to God. Then your sins will be wiped away. The time will come when the Lord will make everything new. He will send the Christ. Jesus has been appointed as the Christ for you. He must remain in heaven until the time when God makes everything new. He promised this long ago through his holy prophets. Moses said, 'The Lord your God will raise up for you a prophet like me. He will be one of your own people. You must listen to everything he tells you. Those who do not listen to him will be completely cut off from their people. *Deuteronomy 18:15,18,19*

"Samuel and all the prophets after him spoke about this. They said these days would come. What the prophets said was meant for you. The covenant God made with your people long ago is yours also. He said to Abraham, 'All nations on earth will be blessed through your children.'—*(Genesis 22:18; 26:4)* God raised up Jesus, who serves him. God sent him first to you. He did it to bless you. He wanted to turn each of you from your evil ways."

Slowly meditate on each verse below. As you feel the presence of the Holy Spirit filling your heart, then Praise Jesus. My example is in verse 3 where He tells me to Publish your book, Bob

Psalm 96 (New Living Translation)

Sing a new song to the Lord!
Let the whole earth sing to the Lord!
Sing to the Lord; praise his name.
Each day proclaim the good news that he saves.
<u>Publish his glorious deeds among the nations,</u>
<u>Tell everyone about the amazing things he does.</u>
Great is the Lord! He is most worthy of praise!
He is to be feared above all gods.
The gods of other nations are mere idols,
but the Lord made the heavens!
Honor and majesty surround him;
strength and beauty fill his sanctuary.

O nations of the world, *recognize* the Lord;
recognize that the Lord is glorious and strong.

Give to the Lord the glory he deserves!
Bring your offering and come into his courts.
Worship the Lord in all his holy splendor.
Let all the earth tremble before him.
Tell all the nations, "The Lord reigns!"
The world stands firm and cannot be shaken.
He will judge all peoples fairly.

Let the heavens be glad, and the earth rejoice!
Let the sea and everything in it shout his praise!
Let the fields and their crops burst out with joy!
Let the trees of the forest rustle with praise
Before the Lord, for he is coming!
He is coming to judge the earth.
He will judge the world with justice,
and the nations with his trut*h*.

The Church's One Foundation
Aurelia

Samuel J. Stone,1839-1900   Samuel Wesley, 1810-1876

1.The Church-'s one foun-da-tion Is Je-sus Christ her Lord;
   She is His New Cre-a-tion, By wa-ter and The Word;
   From heav'n He came and sought her to be His holy bride;
   With His own blood He bought her, and for her life He died.

2. E – lect from ev –'ry nation, yet one o'er all the earth,
   Her charter of sal – va- tion One Lord, one faith, one birth;
   One ho-ly name she blesses, Par – takes one ho – ly food,
   And to one hope she presses, With ev – 'ry grace en - dued.

3. 'Mid toil and trib –u – la – tion and tu – mult of her war,
   She waits the con – sum – ma – tion of peace for –ev – er – more
   Till with the vision glo – rious Her long – ing eyes are blest,
   And the great Church vic –to -rious Shall be the Church at rest.

4. Yet she on earth hath un – ion With God the Three in One,
   And Mistic sweet com –mun – ion With those whose rest is won
   O hap – py ones and holy ! Lord, give us grace that we,
   Like them, the meek and low – ly, On high may dwell with thee.

John 3 (Today's New International Version)

Jesus Teaches Nicodemus

Now there was a Pharisee, a man named Nicodemus who was a member of the
Jewish ruling council.

He came to Jesus at night and said, "Rabbi, we know that you are a teacher who has
come from God. For no one could perform the signs you are doing if God were not
with him."

Jesus replied, "Very truly I tell you, no one can see the kingdom of God
without being born again.

"How can anyone be born when they are old?" Nicodemus asked. "Surely they
cannot enter a second time into their mother's womb to be born!"

Jesus answered, "Very truly I tell you, no one can enter the kingdom of
God without being born of water and the Spirit.

Flesh gives birth to flesh, but the Spirit gives birth to spirit.

You should not be surprised at my saying, 'You must be born again.'

The wind blows wherever it pleases. You hear its sound, but you cannot tell where
it comes from or where it is going. So it is with everyone born of the Spirit."

"How can this be?" Nicodemus asked.

"You are Israel's teacher," said Jesus, "and do you not understand these things?

Very truly I tell you, we speak of what we know, and we testify to what we have
seen, but still you people do not accept our testimony.

I have spoken to you of earthly things and you do not believe; how then will you
believe if I speak of heavenly things?

No one has ever gone into heaven except the one who came from heaven—the
Son man.

Just as Moses lifted up the snake in the wilderness, so the Son of Man must
Be lifted up that everyone who believes may have eternal life in him."

For God so loved the world that he gave his one and only Son, that whoever
believes in him shall not perish but have eternal life.

For God did not send his Son into the world to condemn the world, but to save the
world through him.

Whoever believes in him is not condemned, but whoever does not believe stands
condemned already because they have not believed in the name of God's one and
only Son.

This is the verdict: Light has come into the world, but people loved darkness
Instead of light because their deeds were evil.

All those who do evil hate the light, and will not come into the light for fear that
Their deeds will be exposed.

**But those who live by the truth come into the light, so that it may be seen
Plainly that what they have done has been done in the sight of God.**

John Testifies Again About Jesus

After this, Jesus and his disciples went out into the Judean countryside, where he.
spent some time with them, and baptized.

Now John also was baptizing at Aenon near Salim, because there was plenty of
water, and people were coming and being baptized.

(This was before John was put in prison.)

An argument developed between some of John's disciples and a certain Jew over
the matter of ceremonial washing.

They came to John and said to him, "Rabbi, that man who was with you on the
other side of the Jordan—the one you testified about—look, he is baptizing, and
everyone is going to him."

To this John replied, "A person can receive only what is given from heaven.

You yourselves can testify that I said, 'I am not the Messiah but am sent ahead of
him.'

The bride belongs to the bridegroom. The friend who attends the bridegroom waits
and listens for him, and is full of joy when he hears the bridegroom's voice. That He must
become greater; I must become less."

joy is mine, and it is now complete.

The one who comes from above is above all; the one who is from the earth
belongs to the earth, and speaks as one from the earth. The one who comes from
heaven is above all.

He testifies to what he has seen and heard, but no one accepts his testimony.

The person who has accepted it has certified that God is truthful.

For the one whom God has sent speaks the words of God, for God [i] gives the Spirit without limit.

The Father loves the Son and has placed everything in his hands.

Whoever believes in the Son has eternal life, but whoever rejects the Son (turns away) will not see life, for God's wrath remains on them.

Take A Walk With Jesus

Do You want to see miracles?..........Live With Jesus In Your Heart

Do you want to see Healings?........................ Give each day to Jesus

Do you want to hear the prophetic word?....Live each day in Jesus

Do you want to preach the word?....Examine & lift up the Trinity

Do you want to see demons cast out?.........Give all the glory to God

Do you want to see the resurrection?.........Give all the glory to God

Faith And Obedience In Action

Have You Invited Jesus Into Your Heart ?

As the Father has loved me, so have I loved you. Now remain in my love. If you obey my commands, you will remain in my love, just as I have obeyed my Father's commands and remain in his love. I have told you this so that my joy may be in you and that your joy may be complete. My command is this: Love each other as I have loved you. Greater love has no-one than this, that he lay down his life for his friends. You are my friends if you do what I command. I no longer call you servants, because a servant does not know his master's business. Instead, I have called you friends, for everything that I learned from my Father I have made known to you. You did not choose me, but I chose you and appointed you to go and bear fruit— fruit that will last. Then the Father will give you whatever you ask in my name. This is my command: Love each other. John 15:9-17

2 Peter 3:10-18 (New International Version - UK)

But the day of the Lord will come like a thief. The heavens will disappear with a roar; the elements will be destroyed by fire, and the earth and everything in it will be laid bare.

Since everything will be destroyed in this way, what kind of people ought you to be? You ought to live holy and godly lives

as you look forward to the day of God and speed its coming. That day will bring about the destruction of the heavens by fire, and the elements will melt in the heat.

But in keeping with his promise we are looking forward to a new heaven and a new earth, the home of righteousness.

Be Steadfast

So then, dear friends, since you are looking forward to this, make every effort to be found spotless, blameless and at peace with him.

Bear in mind that our Lord's patience means salvation, just as our dear brother Paul also wrote to you with the wisdom that God gave him.

He writes the same way in all his letters, speaking in them of these matters. His letters contain some things that are hard to understand, which ignorant and unstable people distort, as they do the other Scriptures, to their own destruction.

Therefore, dear friends, since you already know this, be on your guard so that you may not be carried away by the error of lawless men and fall from your secure position.

But grow in the grace and knowledge of our Lord and Savior Jesus Christ. To him be glory both now and for ever! Amen.

.....Face To Face With Jesus !.....

Do you not know that in a race all the runners run, but only one gets the prize? Run in such a way as to get the prize.

Everyone who competes in the games goes into strict training. They do it to get a crown that will not last; but we do it to get a crown that will last forever. Therefore I do not run like a man running aimlessly; I do not fight like a man beating the air. No, I beat my body and make it my slave so that after I have preached to others, I myself will not be disqualified for the prize. 1st Corinthians 9:24-27

.....Face To Face With Jesus !.....Continued

But if I were you, I would appeal to God;
I would lay my cause before him.

He performs wonders that cannot be fathomed,
miracles that cannot be counted.

He bestows rain on the earth;
he sends water on the countryside.

The lowly he sets on high,
and those who mourn are lifted to safety.

He thwarts the plans of the crafty,
so that their hands achieve no success.

He catches the wise in their craftiness,
and the schemes of the wily are swept away.

Darkness comes upon them in the daytime;
at noon they grope as in the night.

He saves the needy from the sword in their mouth;
he saves them from the clutches of the powerful.

So the poor have hope,
and injustice shuts its mouth.

Blessed are those whom God corrects;
so do not despise the discipline of the Almighty.

For he wounds, but he also binds up;
he injures, but his hands also heal.

From six calamities he will rescue you;
in seven no harm will touch you.

In famine he will deliver you from death,
and in battle from the stroke of the sword.

You will be protected from the lash of the tongue,
and need not fear when destruction comes.

You will laugh at destruction and famine,
and need not fear the wild animals.

For you will have a covenant with the stones of the field,
and the wild animals will be at peace with you.

You will know that your tent is secure;
you will take stock of your property and find nothing missing.

You will know that your children will be many,
and your descendants like the grass of the earth.

You will come to the grave in full vigor,
like sheaves gathered in season.

We have examined this, and it is true.
So hear it and apply it to yourself..... Job 5:8-27

Still on some points I have written to you the more boldly and unreservedly by way of reminder. [I have done so] because of the grace (the unmerited favor) bestowed on me by God. Romans 15:15

A New Heaven and a New Earth

Revelation 21

[1] Then I saw "a new heaven and a new earth," for the first heaven and the first earth had passed away, and there was no longer any sea. [2] I saw the Holy City, the new Jerusalem, coming down out of heaven from God, prepared as a bride beautifully dressed for her husband. [3] And I heard a loud voice from the throne saying, "Look! God's dwelling place is now among the people, and he will dwell with them. They will be his people, and God himself will be with them and be their God. [4] 'He will wipe every tear from their eyes. There will be no more death' or mourning or crying or pain, for the old order of things has passed away."

[5] He who was seated on the throne said, "I am making everything new!" Then he said, "Write this down, for these words are trustworthy and true."

[6] He said to me: "It is done. I am the Alpha and the Omega, the Beginning and the End. To the thirsty I will give water without cost from the spring of the water of life. [7] Those who are victorious will inherit all this, and I will be their God and they will be my children. [8] But the cowardly, the unbelieving, the vile, the murderers, the sexually immoral, those who practice magic arts, the idolaters and all liars—they will be consigned to the fiery lake of burning sulfur. This is the second death."

The New Jerusalem, the Bride of the Lamb

⁹ One of the seven angels who had the seven bowls full of the seven last plagues came and said to me, "Come, I will show you the bride, the wife of the Lamb." ¹⁰ And he carried me away in the Spirit to a mountain great and high, and showed me the Holy City, Jerusalem, coming down out of heaven from God. ¹¹ It shone with the glory of God, and its brilliance was like that of a very precious jewel, like a jasper, clear as crystal. ¹² It had a great, high wall with twelve gates, and with twelve angels at the gates. On the gates were written the names of the twelve tribes of Israel. ¹³ There were three gates on the east, three on the north, three on the south and three on the west. ¹⁴ The wall of the city had twelve foundations, and on them were the names of the twelve apostles of the Lamb.

¹⁵ The angel who talked with me had a measuring rod of gold to measure the city, its gates and its walls. ¹⁶ The city was laid out like a square, as long as it was wide. He measured the city with the rod and found it to be 12,000 stadia in length, and as wide and high as it is long. ¹⁷ He measured its wall and it was 144 cubits thick, by human measurement, which the angel was using. ¹⁸ The wall was made of jasper, and the city of pure gold, as pure as glass. ¹⁹ The foundations of the city walls were decorated with every kind of precious stone. The first foundation was jasper, the second sapphire, the third agate, the fourth emerald, ²⁰ the fifth onyx, the sixth ruby, the seventh chrysolite, the eighth beryl, the ninth topaz, the tenth turquoise, the eleventh jacinth, and the twelfth amethyst. ²¹ The twelve gates were twelve pearls, each gate made of a single pearl. The great street of the city was of gold, as pure as transparent glass. ²² I did not see a temple in the city, because the Lord God Almighty and the Lamb are its temple. ²³ The city does not need the sun or the moon to shine on it, for the glory of God gives it light, and the Lamb is its lamp. ²⁴ The nations will walk by its light, and the kings of the earth will bring their splendor into it. ²⁵ On no day will its gates ever be shut, for there will be no night there. ²⁶ The glory and honor of the nations will be brought into it. ²⁷ Nothing impure will ever enter it, nor will anyone who does what is shameful or deceitful, but only those whose names are written in the Lamb's book of life.

Family Gathering

Family Gathering For Christmas

Bob and Sylvia

Large picture on previous page from left to right in the front row: Addison, Ella, Twin daughters of Brenda, Next: Jacob & Julia. (Scott and Dee's children.) Second row: Emma, (Brian and Lori) Benjamin (Dennis and Linda) and Michael. (Brad and Sue)

167

Third row: Dennis, Andrew,(Brad and Sue) Brayden,(Brenda) Bob, Sylvia, Doug, Anna Beth, (Brad and Sue) and Dee,

Fourth row: Samuel & Linda, Brian, Lori, Sue, Katie,(Scott & Dee) Brenda, Kris, Scott.

Back row: Brad, Dave and Rita.....10-27-08

This salvation that we rejoice in was something even the prophets wanted to know more about when they prophesied about this gracious salvation prepared for you. They wondered what time or situation the Spirit of Christ within them was talking about when he told them in advance about Christ's suffering and his great glory afterward.

They were told that their messages were not for themselves, but for you. And now this Good News has been announced to you by those who preached in the power of the Holy Spirit sent from heaven. It is all so wonderful that even the angels are eagerly watching these things happen.

Rejoice

Jesus

My Prince of Peace!

Though He Slay me, Yet I Will Hope In Him; Job 13:15a

Come Lord Jesus! *I am so thankful that you have opened your word in such a tender way, that even I, and hopefully many others will see the tremendous price you paid to redeem us, and hopefully everyone will join in the chorus of Born Again Believers to live triumphantly for you; to be together, gloriously proclaiming your name forever.*

You may have feelings that you would like to share. If so, please, I ask you to mail them to me at the following address:

Bob Bowman

503 7th Street N W

Waverly, Iowa 50677

Or email me at

aclife@mchsi.com

You may also order more books through these same links at the following prices, which will include delivery.

Listing for private sale only. Retail sales will differ.

Less than 10 books……………………………………………$18.00 each

10-20 ……………………………………………………$17.00

20-Up………………………………………………… $16.00

Although I am a gentile, I came into the Kingdom of God when Jesus told me: You must be born again, then I heard Him say, I tell you the truth, Bob, unless you are born again, you cannot see the Kingdom Of God. That day when He spoke those words to me I was so confused as I listened. Then Jesus replied, "I assure you, Bob, no one can enter the Kingdom Of God without being born of water and the Spirit. Humans can reproduce only human life, but the Holy Spirit gives birth to spiritual life. (Not beyond anyone's understanding, Bob) So don't be surprised when I say, You must be born again. The wind blows wherever it wants. Just as you can hear the wind but can't tell where it comes from or where it is going, so you can't explain how people are born of the Spirit." (What can I do, Lord Jesus.) Check out Revelation 3:19-20, and certainly John 3:3-8. These instructions were not given immediate attention, but they enlarged my spirit of understanding, and bless the Lord He never released me until the narrow road became clear.

*(ie. Water and the Spirit: Trusting in <u>His shed blood</u> **for you**, then seeking baptismal water to seal it)*
Because of that, I gave my life to Him in order to declare His gift, which came through a traumatic event.

Acknowledgements

With A Special Thanks To,

My wife Sylvia, for her almost 51 years of faithfulness, her patience, love and devotion, and her partnership in Christ Jesus. To our seven children, their wives, and children for responding to God's Love in Christ Jesus. I love you !

I very much appreciated the help of Betty Bast. You are so special in my life, in union with Christ Jesus. Your editing talents. Christian fellowship, and the joy of working with you will long be remembered. I praise Jesus for the contribution you have made in this book, "A Chosen Life Study."

Also for the Pastoral insights and guidance from Reverend Marvin Talamantez who is the Lead Pastor at Waverly Open Bible. For the congregation of saints who diligently seek God for His will and His way.

Please visit: Amelia Anne's

A Little-bit-of-Heaven site. It is delightful!

Also my personal Christian friends and bible students, Harold Klossowsky for his insights, his Imagery and prose. And who could forget the love and friendship of Susan Shaw and Jim Austin, for their insights and contributions for the books publishing. I praise the Lord Jesus for sending His Spirit to them.

I like to take this opportunity also to thank Melissa Jacobs for her work at The Printery in Waverly, Iowa, as well as the others there who cooperated so politely.

Oren Phipps for his likable and contributing efforts to make this book truly a work for the Holy Father, Son, and Spirit.

This book would not be the same without those who love God and wanted to share their many gifts and handiwork. He blessed them with many talents and they used them well. I praise God Almighty for the printing of this book. It is His, and He is worthy of all the glory.